74

FOUR KEY
CONCEPTS OF THE
QUR'ĀN

FOUR KEY
CONCEPTS OF THE
QUR'ĀN

Sayyid Abul A'lā Mawdūdī

Translated and Edited by Tarik Jan

THE ISLAMIC FOUNDATION

Published by

The Islamic Foundation

Markfield Conference Centre
Ratby Lane, Markfield
Leicestershire, LE67 9SY, United Kingdom
Tel: 01530 244944/5, Fax: 01530 244946
E-mail: info@islamic-foundation.org.uk
publications@islamic-foundation.com
Website: www.islamic-foundation.org.uk

Quran House, P.O. Box 30611, Nairobi, Kenya

P.M.B. 3193, Kano, Nigeria

Copyright © The Islamic Foundation, 2006/1427 H

British Library Cataloguing-in-Publication Data

Mawdudi, Syed Abul Ala, 1903-1979
    Four key concepts of the Qur'an
    1. Koran – commentaries
    I. Title II. Jan, Tarik III. Islamic Foundation (Great Britain)
    297.1'226

ISBN 0 86037 540 4

Printed and bound in England by Antony Rowe Ltd, Chippenham, Wiltshire

Cover/Book design & typeset: Nasir Cadir

Contents

Transliteration Table

Arabic Consonants:

Initial, unexpressed medial and final:

ء	ʾ		د	d		ض	ḍ		ك	k
ب	b		ذ	dh		ط	ṭ		ل	l
ت	t		ر	r		ظ	ẓ		م	m
ث	th		ز	z		ع	ʿ		ن	n
ج	j		س	s		غ	gh		ه	h
ح	ḥ		ش	sh		ف	f		و	w
خ	kh		ص	ṣ		ق	q		ي	y

Vowels, diphthongs, etc.

Short: َ a   ِ i   ُ u

Long: َا ā   ُو ū   ِي ī

Diphthongs: ـَوْ aw

                ـَىْ ay

Foreword

THE MUSLIM *Ummah* is passing through a critical phase. This is not something new as its entire history is characterized by challenges and responses, crisis and re-emergence, relapse and revival. In a sense, this was inevitable. A message as universal and eternal as Islam cannot escape challenges that come with the passage of time and consequent crisis situations. As such it is only through phases of retreat and renewal, and in some cases even disintegration and re-consolidation that an eternal message can remain relevant and a pace-setter for new situations. It was also unavoidable because the very divine arrangement for humans as God's *Khalīfah* (Vicegerent) endowed them with freedom and discretion, hence the prospect of error and correction. Built in the Islamic scheme are elements that are permanent and unchangeable, and as such, constitute the reference points for the system for all times. Along with these are elements that are flexible and changeable, still remaining within the Divinely laid ethos of the system. The sensitive equation between the permanent and the changing sets the evolutionary path of Islam in history. That is how every set-back has been followed by an upsurge throughout the Islamic history. Islam has been the source of every effort at renewal and reassertion.

Today's situation has great similarity with the scenario faced by the *Ummah* at the beginning of the twentieth century, some significant differences notwithstanding. By the end of the nineteenth century, the Muslim *Ummah*, which had played a distinguished role as a world power for over a millennium, was then totally overwhelmed by the forces of decay within and the onslaughts of ascending European imperialisms from abroad. The power-equation changed to the utter disadvantage of the Muslim World. It had far-reaching consequences for the entire realm of Muslim civilization. Western imperial powers represented a new civilizational paradigm. The expansionist role of the imperial powers that vitiated Islam's hold on social dynamics defined its predicament: the Muslims had lost their leading edge over knowledge and technology, their economies were in a shambles, their political power eclipsed. Even morally, culturally and intellectually the *Ummah* went into a tailspin. The lowest point was the abolition in 1924 of what was left of the symbolic *khilāfah*.

This was the context in which a number of Muslim luminaries all over the world addressed themselves to the crucial questions of what had gone wrong with the Muslim *Ummah*? Had Islam become irrelevant or was something wrong with the Muslim approach to Islam, its role in history, in short the way the Muslims were treating the Divine guidance? And finally how the *Ummah* could reset itself along the path to revival and reconstruction? Jamāl al-dīn Afghānī, Amīr Shakīb Arsalān, Prince Ḥalīm Pāshā, Saʿīd Nūrsī, Muḥammad Iqbāl, Rashīd Riḍā', Muḥammad ʿAbduh, Ḥasan al-Bannā, Ashraf ʿAlī Thānawī, Abul Kalām Āzād, Abul Aʿlā Mawdūdī, Mālik bin Nabī, Abul Ḥasan ʿAlī Nadwī and a host of intellectuals and reformers reflected on these questions and came up with positive responses to steer the *Ummah* out of decay. In this galaxy of thinkers and reformers, Mawdūdī occupies a distinct position. Hardly seventeen, in 1920 he initiated the task of rebuilding the Muslim *Ummah*. After ten years of journalistic encounters, he decided to begin his endeavour to reconstruct Muslim thought and to spell out Islam as a worldview and a way of life. His aim was to develop a comprehensive plan of action for the *Ummah*'s revival as a blessing for humanity. The publication of *al-Jihād fī al-Islām* (law of War and Peace in Islam) in 1929 was his first such major contribution. And ever since, until his death on 22nd September, 1979, he authored over 140 books and tracts on Islam, covering almost every aspect of its thought and message. His greatest work is a six-volume exegesis of the Qur'ān —*Tafhīm al-Qur'ān* — spanning several thousand pages. Besides articulation and reconstruction of Islamic thought, he developed a critique of the Muslim society, identifying the causes of their decline. His effort was to make the Muslims realize how and why they lost their grip on their own affairs, resulting in political, economic and intellectual decline. He also came up with a powerful critique of the Western civilization, the main player in the contemporary onslaught on Islam. He was not oblivious to the positive achievements of the Western civilization, the sources of its strength and weakness and the ideologies it had spun. But at the same time, he was critical of its intellectual confusion, its moral deprivations, its political and cultural deformities and its economic injustices and exploitations. His thought has influenced three generations of Muslims. Small wonder he is considered as one of the chief architects of contemporary Islamic revival.

Mawdūdī, along with being a great thinker and a visionary, was also a reformer and an activist committed to strive for social change and historic transformation. He founded in 1941, for moral and socio-economic change, the Jamāʿat-e-Islāmī, a movement to pilot Islamic resurgence, initially in the South Asian Sub-continent, but ultimately as part of a global movement for the establishment of a just world order.

The need for translating Mawdūdī's essential writings into the English language was never as pressing as it is today. The translations I did in the 1960s and those that Br. Khurram Murad did in the 1980s cover hardly twenty percent of his work. The World of Islam Trust, Islamabad, the Islamic Research Academy, Karachi and the Islamic Foundation, Leicester have now agreed to co-sponsor English translations of his essential works. The manuscripts would be prepared under my general supervision and editorship, assisted by Dr. Anis Ahmad, Dr. Manazir Ahsan and Dr. A.R. Kidwai. Tarik Jan and Shafaq Hashemi would do the major work of translation and compilation. Other competent translators would also be involved in this project. The Madinah Trust, Peterborough, and the Sarwar Jehan Charitable

Foundation, Leicester, U.K. are also extending some limited financial support for the project.

Our vision is that except those of Mawdūdī's writings which were of local or very contemporaneous concern, the remainder of his work should be available to English readers followed by translations in other languages of the world. Except the Arabic, Persian, Hindi, and Bengali versions, which were largely prepared from the original Urdu text, the other translations in over twenty-five languages were made from their English and Arabic versions. The idea is that what Mawdūdī (*raḥimahullāh*) wrote in the twentieth century should be made available to the *Ummah* for its guidance in the twenty-first century, at least as a window on the Islamic revivalist movement of the twentieth century and as a searchlight for the vista of the new millennium. This work may also provide an opportunity to others for further development and adaptation of Islamic concepts and strategies in view of the changing circumstances and new challenges. Every human being, however great, has his limitations. Yet what Mawdūdī wrote over a period of sixty years remains of everlasting relevance to the issues and problems of Islamic resurgence and reconstruction of Muslim Society and culture in the face of new challenges. The works of Mawdūdī are important both in view of their thought-content as well as a way of looking at the message and meaning of Islam in view of changing circumstances. His contribution is relevant as datum as well as methodology. We hope to complete the project in sixteen or more volumes. A tentative list of themes for these volumes is given below:

- Vol. 1 – Islam: Message and Movement – This would cover selected chapters from *Islāmī niẓām-i zindagī*.

- Vol. 2 – Islam: Faith as the Basis of Culture – Translation of *Islāmī tahdhīb aur uskay uṣūl wa mabādī*.

- Vol. 3 – Four Key Concepts of the Qur'ān – Translation of *Qur'ān kī chār bunyādī iṣṭilāḥayn* and other relevant articles.

- Vol. 4 – Islamic Movement – Selected articles on the concept of Islamic movement, its methodology and strategy for change.

- Vol. 5 – Islamic Movement: Sources of Spirituality – Covering the fields of *'ibādah, tazkiyah* and *Iḥsān.*

- Vol. 6 – Worship in Islam – Concept of *'ibādah* and deeper look at *Ṣalāh* (Prayer) and *Ṣawm* (Fast)

- Vol. 7 – Islam and the Secular Mind – Selections from *Tanqīḥāt* and *Tafhīmāt*, dealing with the challenge from secular civilizations.

- Vol. 8 – Islamic Law. (Selected Writings)

- Vol. 9 – Islamic State. (Selected Writings)

- Vol. 10 – Islamic Economics. (Selected Writings)

- Vol. 11 – Islamic Culture and Society. (Selected Writings)

- Vol. 12 – Revival and Renovation in Islam: Concept and History.

- Vol. 13 – Caliphate and Monarchy in Islamic History: Translation of *Khilāfat wa mulūkīyat.*

- Vol. 14 – Law of War and Peace in Islam.

- Vol. 15 – Islamic Thought and Practice: Selected chapters from *Tafhīmāt* (all the five volumes).

- Vol. 16 – Islamic Discourses: Selections from *Rasā'il wa Masā'il* (five volumes) and interviews and speeches dealing with contemporary issues – conceptual, civilizational and behavioural.

These volumes are not planned to appear in the preceding sequence. Nor is it suggested that the volumes would necessarily have the titles given above. Nevertheless, this framework is being sketched to give readers an idea of the scope of this work and the richness of the themes expected to be covered. The volumes could appear, as and when they are ready. The volume we are now in a position to offer in the series is *Four Key Concepts of the Qur'ān*, which has been very ably translated and edited by my brother and colleague Tarik Jan. I pray to Allah to bless him with the best of rewards for his labour of love.

Sayyid Mawdūdī's introduction to *Tafhīm al-Qur'ān* has also been included in this volume as a general introduction to the more focused discussion on the concepts of *ilāh*, *Rabb*, *dīn* and *'ibādah*.

Before I conclude I would like to place on record my appreciation for the support and valuable assistance received from my brothers and colleagues Zafar Ishaq Ansari, Anis Ahmad, Muhammad Manazir Ahsan, A.R. Kidwai, Khalid Rahman, Ziaul Hasan and Shiraz Gul, Anwar Cara, Naiem Qaddoura and Nasir Cadir for the valuable assistance they provided in enabling the project to see the light of day. May Allah reward them all for their efforts in His cause.

Islamabad   **Khurshid Ahmad**
3rd Dhu'l Ḥijjah 1426 A.H.
4th January 2006

Introduction[1]

IT MUST be said at once that this is an introduction to *Towards Understanding the Qur'ān*, and not to the Qur'ān itself. It has been written with two objectives. First, to acquaint the reader with certain matters which he should grasp at the very outset so as to achieve a more than superficial understanding of the Holy Book. Second, to clarify those disturbing questions that commonly arise in the mind of the reader during the study of the Qur'ān.

[I]

We are accustomed to reading books which present information, ideas and arguments systematically and coherently. So when we embark on the study of the Qur'ān, we expect that this book too will revolve around a definite subject, that the subject matter of the book will be clearly defined at the beginning and will then be neatly divided into sections and chapters, after which discussion will proceed in a logical sequence. We likewise expect a separate and systematic arrangement of instruction and guidance for each of the various aspects of human life.

---

1. Mawlānā Abul A'lā Mawdūdī wrote this 'Introduction' for his *Tafhīm al-Qur'ān*. It is being reproduced here to acquaint the readers with some of the basic ideas that inform the author's approach to understanding the Qur'ān. Tr.

However, as soon as we open the Qur'ān we encounter a hitherto completely unfamiliar genre of literature. We notice that it embodies precepts of belief and conduct, moral directives, legal prescriptions, exhortation and admonition, censure and condemnation of evildoers, warnings to deniers of the Truth, good tidings and words of consolation and good cheer to those who have suffered for the sake of God, arguments and corroborative evidence in support of its basic message, allusions to anecdotes from the past and to signs of God visible in the universe. Moreover, these myriad subjects alternate without any apparent system; quite unlike the books to which we are accustomed, the Qur'ān deals with the same subject over and over again, each time couched in a different phraseology.

The reader also encounters abrupt transitions between one subject matter and another. Audience and speaker constantly change as the message is directed now to one and now to another group of people. There is no trace of the familiar division into chapters and sections. Likewise, the treatment of different subjects is unique. If an historical subject is raised, the narrative does not follow the pattern familiar in historical accounts. In discussions of philosophical or metaphysical questions, we miss the familiar expressions and terminology of formal logic and philosophy. Cultural and political matters, or questions pertaining to man's social and economic life, are discussed in a way very different from that usual in works of social sciences. Juristic principles and legal injunctions are elucidated, but quite differently from the manner of conventional works. When we come across an ethical instruction, we find its form differs entirely from anything to be found elsewhere in the literature of ethics.

The reader may find all this so foreign to his notion of what a book should be that he may become so confused as to feel that the Qur'ān is a piece of disorganized, incoherent and unsystematic writing, comprising nothing but a disjointed conglomeration of comments of varying lengths put together arbitrarily. Hostile critics use this as a basis for their criticism, while those more favourably inclined resort to far-fetched explanations, or else conclude that the Qur'ān consists of unrelated pieces, thus making it amenable to all kinds of interpretation,

even interpretations quite opposed to the intent of God Who revealed
the Book.

[II]

What kind of book, then, is the Qur'ān? In what manner was it
revealed? What underlies its arrangement? What is its subject? What
is its true purpose? What is the central theme to which its multifarious
topics are intrinsically related? What kind of reasoning and style does
it adopt in elucidating its central theme? If we could obtain clear,
lucid answers to these and other related questions we might avoid
some dangerous pitfalls, thus making it easier to reflect upon and to
grasp the meaning and purpose of the Qur'ānic verses. If we begin
studying the Qur'ān in the expectation of reading a book on religion
we shall find it hard, since our notions of religion and of a book
are naturally circumscribed by our range of experience. We need,
therefore, to be told in advance that this Book is unique in the manner
of its composition, in its theme and in its contents and arrangement.
We should be forewarned that the concept of a book which we have
formed from our previous readings is likely to be a hindrance, rather
than a help, towards a deep understanding of the Qur'ān. We should
realize that as a first step towards understanding it we must disabuse
our minds of all preconceived notions.

[III]

The student of the Qur'ān should grasp, from the outset, the
fundamental claims that the Qur'ān makes for itself. Whether one
ultimately decides to believe in the Qur'ān or not, one must recognize
the fundamental statements made by the Qur'ān and by the man to
whom it was revealed, the Prophet Muḥammad (peace be on him), to
be the starting point of one's study. These claims are:

1. The Lord of creation, the Creator and Sovereign of the entire
universe, created man on earth (which is merely a part of His

boundless realm). He also endowed man with the capacity for cognition, reflection and understanding, with the ability to distinguish between good and evil, with the freedom of choice and volition, and with the power to exercise his latent potentialities. In short, God bestowed upon man a kind of autonomy and appointed him His vicegerent on earth.

2. Although man enjoys this status, God made it abundantly plain to him that He alone is man's Lord and Sovereign, even as He is the Lord and Sovereign of the whole universe. Man was told that he was not entitled to consider himself independent and that only God was entitled to claim absolute obedience, service and worship. It was also made clear to man that life in this world, for which he had been placed and invested with a certain honour and authority, was in fact a temporary term, and was meant to test him; that after the end of this earthly life man must return to God, Who will judge him on the basis of his performance, declaring who has succeeded and who has failed.

The right way for man is to regard God as his only Sovereign and the only object of his worship and adoration, to follow the guidance revealed by God, to act in this world in the consciousness that earthly life is merely a period of trial, and to keep his eyes fixed on the ultimate objective – success in God's final judgement. Every other way is wrong.

It was also explained to man that if he chose to adopt the right way of life – and in this choice he was free – he would enjoy peace and contentment in this world and be assigned, on his return to God, the abode of eternal bliss and happiness known as Paradise. Should man follow any other way – and he was free to do so – he would experience the evil effects of corruption and disorder in the life of this world and be consigned to eternal grief and torment when he crossed the borders of the present world and arrived in the Hereafter.

3. Having explained all this, the Lord of the Universe placed man on earth and communicated to Adam and Eve, the first human beings

to live on earth, the guidance which they and their offspring were required to follow. These first human beings were not born in a state of ignorance and darkness. On the contrary, they began their life in the broad daylight of Divine Guidance. They had intimate knowledge of reality and the Law which they were to follow was communicated to them. Their way of life consisted of obedience to God (i.e. Islam) and they taught their children to live in obedience to Him (i.e. to live as Muslims).

In the course of time, however, men gradually deviated from this true way of life and began to follow various erroneous ways. They allowed true guidance to be lost through heedlessness and negligence and sometimes, even deliberately, distorted it out of evil perversity. They associated with God a number of beings, human and non-human, real as well as imaginary, and adored them as deities. They adulterated the God-given knowledge of reality, (al-'ilm in the Qur'ānic terminology), with all kinds of fanciful ideas, superstitions and philosophical concepts, thereby giving birth to innumerable religions. They disregarded or distorted the sound and equitable principles of individual morality and of collective conduct (al-Sharī'ah in the Qur'ānic terminology) and made their own laws in accordance with their base desires and prejudices. As a result, the world became filled with wrong and injustice.

4. It was inconsistent with the limited autonomy conferred upon man by God that He should exercise His overwhelming power and compel man to righteousness. It was also inconsistent with the fact that God had granted a term to the human species in which to show their worth that He should afflict men with catastrophic destruction as soon as they showed signs of rebellion. Moreover, God had undertaken from the beginning of creation that true guidance would be made available to man throughout the term granted to him and that this guidance would be available in a manner consistent with man's autonomy. To fulfil this self-assumed responsibility God chose to appoint those human beings whose faith in Him was outstanding and who followed the way pleasing to Him. God chose these people to be His envoys.

He had His messages communicated to them, honoured them with an intimate knowledge of reality, provided them with the true laws of life and entrusted them with the task of recalling man to the original path from which he had strayed.[2]

5. These Prophets were sent to different people in different lands and over a period of time covering thousands and thousands of years. They all had the same religion; the one originally revealed to man as the right way for him. All of them followed the same guidance; those principles of morality and collective life prescribed for man at the very outset of his existence. All these Prophets had the same mission – to call man to this true religion and subsequently to organize all who accepted this message into a community (*ummah*) which would be bound by the Law of God, which would strive to establish its observance and would seek to prevent its violation. All the Prophets discharged their missions creditably in their own time. However, there were always many who refused to accept their guidance and consequently those who did accept it and became a 'Muslim' community[3] gradually degenerated, causing the Divine Guidance either to be lost, distorted or adulterated.

6. At last the Lord of the Universe sent Muḥammad (peace be on him) to Arabia and entrusted him with the same mission that He had entrusted to the earlier Prophets. This last Messenger of God addressed the followers of the earlier Prophets (who had by this time deviated from their original teachings) as well as the rest of humanity. The mission of each Prophet was to call men to the right way of life, to communicate God's true guidance afresh and to organize into one community all who responded to his mission and accepted the guidance vouchsafed to him. Such a community was to be dedicated

---

2. These men were Prophets and Messengers of God. Tr.

3. That is, a group of people committed to obey the true guidance of God as revealed to His Prophets. Here the word "Muslim" is not used in the sense of followers of the last Messenger of God, Muḥammad (peace be on him), but in the wider sense, meaning all those who, at various periods, both before and after the advent of the Last Prophet, committed themselves to live in submission to God. Tr.

to the two-fold task of moulding its own life in accordance with God's guidance and striving for the reform of the world. The Qur'ān is the Book which embodies this mission and guidance revealed by God to Muḥammad (peace be on him).

[IV]

If we remember these basic facts about the Qur'ān it becomes easy to grasp its true subject, its central theme and the objective it seeks to achieve. Insofar as it seeks to explain the ultimate causes of man's success or failure the subject of the Book is MAN.

Its central theme is that concepts relating to God, the universe and man which have emanated from man's own limited knowledge run counter to reality. The same applies to concepts which have been either woven by man's intellectual fancies or which have evolved through man's obsession with animal desires. The ways of life which rest on these false foundations are both contrary to reality and ruinous for man. The essence of true knowledge is that which God revealed to man when He appointed him His vicegerent. Hence, the way of life which is in accordance with reality and conducive to human good is that which we have characterized above as 'the right way'. The real object of the Book is to call people to this 'right way' and to illuminate God's true guidance, which has often been lost either through man's negligence and heedlessness or distorted by his wicked perversity.

If we study the Qur'ān with these facts in mind it is bound to strike us that the Qur'ān does not deviate one iota from its main subject, its central theme and its basic objective. All the various themes occurring in the Qur'ān are related to the central theme; just as beads of different sizes and colour may be strung together to form a necklace. The Qur'ān speaks of the structure of the heavens and the earth and of man, refers to the signs of reality in the various phenomena of the universe, relates anecdotes of bygone nations, criticizes the beliefs, morals and deeds of different peoples, elucidates supernatural truths and discusses many other things besides. All this the Qur'ān does, not in order to provide instruction in physics, history, philosophy or any other particular branch of knowledge, but rather to remove the misconceptions people have about reality and to make that reality manifest to them.

It emphasizes that the various ways men follow, which are not in conformity with reality, are essentially false, and full of harmful consequences for mankind. It calls on men to shun all such ways and to follow instead the way which both conforms to reality and yields the best practical results. This is why the Qur'ān mentions everything only to the extent and in the manner necessary for the purposes it seeks to serve. The Qur'ān confines itself to essentials thereby omitting any irrelevant details. Thus, all its contents consistently revolve around this call.

Likewise, it is not possible fully to appreciate either the style of the Qur'ān, the order underlying the arrangement of its verses or the diversity of the subjects treated in it, without fully understanding the manner in which it was revealed.

The Qur'ān, as we have noted earlier, is not a book in the conventional sense of the term. God did not compose and entrust it in one piece to Muḥammad (peace be on him) so that he could spread its message and call people to adopt an attitude to life consonant with its teachings. Nor is the Qur'ān one of those books which discusses their subjects and main themes in the conventional manner. Its arrangement differs from that of ordinary books, and its style is correspondingly different. The nature of this Book is that God chose a man in Makkah to serve as His Messenger and asked him to preach His message, starting in his own city (Makkah) and with his own tribe (Quraysh). At this initial stage, instructions were confined to what was necessary at this particular juncture of the mission. Three themes in particular stand out:

1. Directives were given to the Prophet (peace be on him) on how he should prepare himself for his great mission and how he should begin working for the fulfilment of his task.

2. A fundamental knowledge of reality was furnished and misconceptions commonly held by people in that regard –

misconceptions which gave rise to wrong orientation in life – were removed.

3. People were exhorted to adopt the right attitude toward life. Moreover, the Qur'ān also elucidated those fundamental principles which, if followed, lead to man's success and happiness.

In keeping with the character of the mission at this stage the early revelations generally consisted of short verses, couched in language of uncommon grace and power, and clothed in a literary style suited to the taste and temperament of the people to whom they were originally addressed, and whose hearts they were meant to penetrate. The rhythm, melody and vitality of these verses drew rapt attention, and such was their stylistic grace and charm that people began to recite them involuntarily.

The local colour of these early messages is conspicuous, for while the truths they contained were universal, the arguments and illustrations used to elucidate them were drawn from the immediate environment familiar to the first listeners. Allusions were made to their history and traditions and to the visible traces of the past which had crept into the beliefs, and into the moral and social life of Arabia. All this was calculated to enhance the appeal the message held for its immediate audience. This early stage lasted for four or five years, during which period the following reactions to the Prophet's message manifested themselves:

1. A few people responded to the call and agreed to join the *ummah* (community) committed, of its own volition, to submit to the Will of God.

2. Many people reacted with hostility, either from out of ignorance or egotism, or because of chauvinistic attachment to the way of life of their forefathers.

3. The call of the Prophet, however, did not remain confined to Makkah or to the Quraysh. It began to meet with favourable response beyond the borders of that city and among other tribes.

The next stage of the mission was marked by a hard, vigorous struggle between the Islamic movement and the age-old Ignorance[4] (*Jāhilīyah*) of Arabia. Not only were the Makkans and the Quraysh bent upon preserving their inherited way of life, they were also firmly resolved to suppress the new movement by force. They stopped at nothing in the pursuit of this objective. They resorted to false propaganda; they spread doubt and suspicion and used subtle, malicious insinuations to sow distrust in people's minds. They tried to prevent people from listening to the message of the Prophet. They perpetrated savage cruelties on those who embraced Islam. They subjected them to economic and social boycott, and persecuted them to such an extent that on two occasions a number of them were forced to leave home and emigrate to Abyssinia, and finally they had to emigrate *en masse* to Madinah.

In spite of this strong and growing resistance and opposition, the Islamic movement continued to spread. There was hardly a family left in Makkah one of whose members at least had not embraced Islam. Indeed, the violence and bitterness of the enemies of Islam was due to the fact that their own kith and kin – brothers, nephews, sons, daughters, sisters, brothers-in-law and so on – had not only embraced Islam, but were even ready to sacrifice their lives for its sake. Their resistance, therefore, brought them into conflict with their own nearest and dearest. Moreover, those who had forsaken the age-old Ignorance of Arabia included many who were outstanding members of their Society. After embracing Islam, they became so remarkable for their moral uprightness, their veracity and their purity of character that the world could hardly fail to notice the superiority of the message which was attracting people of such qualities.

---

4. The author uses the term 'Ignorance' (*Jāhilīyah*) to denote all those world-views and ways of life which are based on the rejection or disregard of the heavenly guidance which is communicated to mankind through the Prophets and Messengers of God; the attitude of treating human life – either wholly or partly – as independent of the directives revealed by God. For this see the writings of the author, especially *Islam and Ignorance* (Lahore: 1976), and *A Short History of the Revivalist Movements in Islam*, tr. al-Ash'ari, III edition (Lahore: 1976). Tr.

During the Prophet's long and arduous struggle God continued to inspire him with revelations possessing at once the smooth, natural flow of a river, the violent force of a flood and the overpowering effect of a fierce fire. These messages instructed the believers in their basic duties, inculcated in them a sense of community and belonging, exhorted them to piety, moral excellence and purity of character, taught them how to preach the true faith, sustained their spirit by promises of success and Paradise in the Hereafter, aroused them to struggle in the cause of God with patience, fortitude and high spirits, and filled their hearts with such zeal and enthusiasm that they were prepared to endure every sacrifice, brave every hardship and face every adversity.

At the same time, those either bent on opposition, or who had deviated from the right way, or who had immersed themselves in frivolity and wickedness, were warned by having their attentions called to the tragic ends of nations with whose fates they were familiar. They were asked to draw lessons from the ruins of those localities through which they passed every day in the course of their wanderings. Evidence for the unity of God and for the existence of the After-life was pointed to in signs visible to their own eyes and within the range of their ordinary experience. The weaknesses inherent in polytheism, the vanity of man's ambition to become independent even of God, the folly of denying the After-life, the perversity of blind adherence to the ways of one's ancestors regardless of right or wrong, were all fully elucidated with the help of arguments cogent enough to penetrate the minds and hearts of the audience.

Moreover, every misgiving was removed, a reasonable answer was provided to every objection, all confusion and perplexity was cleared up, and Ignorance was besieged from all sides till its irrationality was totally exposed. Along with all this went the warning of the wrath of God. The people were reminded of the horrors of Doomsday and the tormenting punishment of Hell. They were also censured for their moral corruption, for their erroneous ways of life, for their clinging to the ways of Ignorance, for their opposition to Truth and their persecution of the believers. Furthermore, these messages enunciated those fundamental principles of morality and collective life on which all sound and healthy civilizations enjoying God's approval had always rested.

This stage was unfolded in several phases. In each phase, the preaching of the message assumed ever-wider proportions, as the struggle for the cause of Islam and opposition to it became increasingly intense and severe, and as the believers encountered people of varying outlooks and beliefs. All these factors had the effect of increasing the variety of the topics treated in the messages revealed during this period. Such, in brief, was the situation forming the background to the Makkan *sūrahs* of the Qur'ān.

[V]

For thirteen years the Islamic movement strove in Makkah. It then obtained, in Madinah, a haven of refuge in which to concentrate its followers and its strength. The Prophet's movement now entered its third stage.

During this stage, circumstances changed drastically. The Muslim community succeeded in establishing a full-fledged state; its creation was followed by prolonged armed conflict with the representatives of the ancient Ignorance of Arabia. The community also encountered followers of the former Prophets, i.e. Jews and Christians. An additional problem was that hypocrites began to join the fold of the Muslim community; their machinations needed to be resisted. After a severe struggle, lasting ten years, the Islamic movement reached a high point of achievement when the entire Arabian peninsula came under its sway and the door was open to world-wide preaching and reform. This stage, like the preceding one, passed through various phases each of which had its peculiar problems and demands.

It was in the context of these problems that God continued to reveal messages to the Prophet. At times these messages were couched in the form of fiery speeches; at other times they were characterized by the grandeur and stateliness of majestic proclamations and ordinances. At times they had the air of instructions from a teacher; at others the style of preaching of a reformer. These messages explained how a healthy society, state and civilization could be established and the principles on which the various aspects of human life should be based.

They also dealt with matters directly related to the specific problems facing the Muslims. For example, how should they deal with the hypocrites (who were harming the Muslim community from within) and with the non-Muslims who were living under the care of the Muslim society? How should they relate to the People of the Book? What treatment should be meted out to those with whom the Muslims were at war, and how should they deal with those with whom they were bound by treaties and agreements? How should the believers, as a community, prepare to discharge their obligations as vicegerents of the Lord of the Universe? Through the Qur'ān the Muslims were guided in questions like these, were instructed and trained, made aware of their weaknesses, urged to risk their lives and property for the cause of God, taught the code of morality they should observe in all circumstances of life – in times of victory and defeat, ease and distress, prosperity and adversity, peace and security, peril and danger.

In short, they were being trained to serve as the successors of the mission of the Prophet, with the task of carrying on the message of Islam and bringing about reform in human life. The Qur'ān also addressed itself to those outside the fold of Islam, to the People of the Book, the hypocrites, the unbelievers, the polytheists. Each group was addressed according to its own particular circumstances and attitudes. Sometimes the Qur'ān invited them to the true faith with tenderness and delicacy; on other occasions, it rebuked and severely admonished them. It also warned them against, and threatened them with, punishment from God. It attempted to make them take heed by drawing their attention to instructive historical events. In short, people were left with no valid reason for refusing the call of the Prophet.

Such, briefly, is the background to the Madinan *sūrahs* of the Qur'ān.

It is now clear to us that the revelation of the Qur'ān began and went hand in hand with the preaching of the message. This message passed through many stages and met with diverse situations from the very beginning and throughout a period of twenty-three years.

The different parts of the Qur'ān were revealed step by step according to the multifarious, changing needs and requirements of the Islamic movement during these stages. It therefore could not possibly possess the kind of coherence and systematic sequence expected of a doctoral dissertation. Moreover, the various fragments of the Qur'ān which were revealed in harmony with the growth of the Islamic movement were not published in the form of written treatises, but were spread orally. Their style, therefore, bore an oratorical flavour rather than the characteristics of literary composition.

Furthermore, these orations were delivered by one whose task meant that he had to appeal simultaneously to the mind, to the heart and to the emotions, and to people of different mental levels and dispositions. He had to revolutionize people's thinking, to arouse in them a storm of noble emotions in support of his cause, to persuade his Companions and inspire them with devotion and zeal, and with the desire to improve and reform their lives. He had to raise their morale and steel their determination, turn enemies into friends and opponents into admirers, disarm those out to oppose his message and show their position to be morally untenable. In short, he had to do everything necessary to carry his movement through to a successful conclusion. Orations revealed in conformity with the requirements of a message and movement will inevitably have a style different from that of a professorial lecture.

This explains the repetitions we encounter in the Qur'ān. The interests of a message and a movement demand that during a particular stage emphasis should be placed only on those subjects which are appropriate at that stage, to the exclusion of matters pertaining to later stages. As a result, certain subjects may require continual emphasis for months or even years. On the other hand, constant repetition in the same manner becomes exhausting. Whenever a subject is repeated, it should therefore be expressed in different phraseology, in new forms and with stylistic variations so as to ensure that the ideas and beliefs being put over find their way into the hearts of the people.

At the same time, it was essential that the fundamental beliefs and principles on which the movement was based should always be kept fresh in people's minds; a necessity which dictated that they should be repeated continually through all stages of the movement. For this reason, certain basic Islamic concepts about the unity of God and His Attributes, about the Hereafter, about man's accountability and about reward and punishment, about prophethood and belief in the revealed scriptures, about basic moral attributes such as piety, patience, trust in God and so on, recur throughout the Qur'ān. If these ideas had lost their hold on the hearts and minds of people, the Islamic movement could not have moved forward in its true spirit.

If we reflect on this, it also becomes evident why the Prophet (peace be on him) did not arrange the Qur'ān in the sequence in which it was revealed. As we have noted, the context in which the Qur'ān was revealed in the course of twenty-three years was the mission and movement of the Prophet; the revelations correspond with the various stages of this mission and movement. Now, it is evident that when the Prophet's mission was completed, the chronological sequence of the various parts of the Qur'ān – revealed in accordance with the growth of the Prophet's mission – could in no way be suitable to the changed situation. What was now required was a different sequence in tune with the changed context resulting from the completion of the mission.

Initially, the Prophet's message was addressed to people totally ignorant of Islam. Their instruction had to start with the most elementary things. After the mission had reached its successful completion, the Qur'ān acquired a compelling relevance for those who had decided to believe in the Prophet. By virtue of that belief they had become a new religious community – the Muslim *ummah*. Not only that, they had been made responsible for carrying on the Prophet's mission, which he had bequeathed to them, in a perfected form on both conceptual and practical levels. It was no longer necessary for the Qur'ānic verses to be arranged in chronological sequence. In the changed context, it had become necessary for the bearers of the mission of the Prophet (peace be on him) to be informed of their duties and of the true principles and laws governing their lives. They also had to be warned against the deviations and corruptions which had appeared among the followers of earlier Prophets. All this was necessary in order to equip the Muslims to go out and offer the light of Divine Guidance to a world steeped in darkness.

It would be foreign to the very nature of the Qur'ān to group together in one place all verses relating to a specific subject; the nature of the Qur'ān requires that the reader should find teachings revealed during the Madinan period interspersed with those of the Makkan period, and vice versa. It requires the juxtaposition of early discourses with instructions from the later period of the life of the Prophet. This blending of teachings from different periods helps to provide an overall view and an integrated perspective of Islam and acts as a safeguard against lopsidedness. Furthermore, a chronological arrangement of the Qur'ān would have been meaningful to later generations only if it had been supplemented with explanatory notes and these would have had to be treated as inseparable appendices to the Qur'ān. This would have been quite contrary to God's purpose in revealing the Qur'ān; the main purpose of its revelation was that all human beings – children and young people, old men and women, town and country dwellers, laymen and scholars – should be able to refer to the Divine Guidance available to them in composite form and providentially secured against adulteration. This was necessary to enable people of every level of intelligence and understanding to know what God required of them. This purpose would have been defeated had the reader been obliged solemnly to recite detailed historical notes and explanatory comments along with the Book of God.

Those who object to the present arrangement of the Qur'ān appear to be suffering from a misapprehension as to its true purpose. They sometimes almost seem under the illusion that it was revealed merely for the benefit of students of history and sociology!

[VI]

The present arrangement of the Qur'ān is not the work of later generations, but was made by the Prophet under God's direction. Whenever a *sūrah* was revealed, the Prophet summoned his scribes, to whom he carefully dictated its contents, and instructed them where to place it in relation to the other *sūrahs*. The Prophet followed the same order of *sūrahs* and verses when reciting during ritual Prayer as on other occasions, and his Companions followed the same practice in memorizing the Qur'ān. It is therefore a historical fact that the collection of the Qur'ān came to an end on the very day that its revelation ceased. The One who was responsible for its revelation was also the One who set its arrangement. The one whose heart was the receptacle of the Qur'ān was also responsible for arranging its sequence. This was far too important and too delicate a matter for anyone else to dare to become involved in.

Since Prayers were obligatory for the Muslims from the very outset of the Prophet's mission,[5] and the recitation of the Qur'ān was an obligatory part of those Prayers, Muslims were committing the Qur'ān to memory while its revelation continued. Thus, as soon as a fragment of the Qur'ān was revealed, it was memorized by some of the Companions. Hence the preservation of the Qur'ān was not solely dependent on its verses being inscribed on palm leaves, pieces of bone, leather and scraps of parchment – the materials used by the Prophet's scribes for writing down Qur'ānic verses. Instead those verses came to be inscribed upon scores, then hundreds, then thousands, then hundreds of thousands of human hearts, soon after they had been revealed, so that no scope was left for any devil to alter so much as one word of them.

When, after the death of the Prophet, the storm of apostasy convulsed Arabia and the Companions had to plunge into bloody battles to suppress it, many Companions who had memorized the Qur'ān

---

5. It should be noted that while the five daily Prayers were made obligatory several years after the Prophet was commissioned, Prayers were obligatory from the very outset; not a single moment elapsed when Prayers, as such, were not obligatory in Islam.

suffered martyrdom. This led ʿUmar to plead that the Qur'ān ought to be preserved in writing, as well as orally. He therefore impressed the urgency of this upon Abū Bakr. After slight hesitation, the latter agreed and entrusted that task to Zayd ibn Thābit al-Anṣārī, who had worked as a scribe of the Prophet.[6]

The procedure decided upon was to try and collect all written pieces of the Qur'ān left behind by the Prophet, as well as those in the possession of his Companions.[7] When all this had been done, assistance was sought from those who had memorized the Qur'ān. No verse was incorporated into the Qur'ānic codex unless all three sources were found to be in complete agreement, and every criterion of verification had been satisfied. Thus an authentic version of the Qur'ān was prepared. It was kept in the custody of Ḥafṣah (a wife of the Holy Prophet) and people were permitted to make copies of it and also to use it as the standard of comparison when rectifying the mistakes they might have made in writing down the Qur'ān.

In different parts of Arabia and among its numerous tribes there existed a diversity of dialects. The Qur'ān was revealed in the language spoken by the Quraysh of Makkah. Nevertheless, in the beginning, people of other areas and other tribes were permitted to recite it according to their own dialects and idiom, since this facilitated its recitation without affecting its substantive meaning. In the course of time, in the wake of the conquest of a sizeable part of the world outside of the Arabian peninsula, a large number of non-Arabs entered the fold of Islam. These developments affected the Arabic idiom and it was feared that the continuing use of various dialects in the recitation of the Qur'ān might give rise to grave problems. It was possible, for

---

6. For an account of the early history of the Qur'ān see Ṣubḥī Ṣāliḥ, *Mabāḥith fī ʿUlūm al-Qur'ān* (Beirut: 1977), pp. 65ff. Tr.

7. There are authentic Traditions to the effect that several Companions had committed the entire Qur'ān, or many parts of it, to writing during the lifetime of the Prophet. Especially mentioned in this connection are the following Companions of the Prophet: ʿUthmān, ʿAlī, ʿAbd Allāh ibn Masʿūd, ʿAbd Allāh ibn ʿAmr ibn al-ʿĀṣ, Sālim the mawlā of Ḥudhayfah, Muʿādh ibn Jabal, Ubayy b. Kaʿb, and Abū Zayd Qays ibn al-Sakan.

instance, that someone hearing the Qur'ān recited in an unfamiliar dialect might pick a fight with the reciter, thinking that the latter was deliberately distorting the Word of God. It was also possible that such differences might gradually lead to tampering with the Qur'ān itself. It was also not inconceivable that the hybridization of the Arabic language, due to the intermixture between Arabs and non-Arabs, might lead people to introduce modifications into the Qur'ānic text, thus impairing the grace of the Speech of God. As a result of such considerations, and after consultation with the Companions of the Prophet, 'Uthmān decided that copies of the standard edition of the Qur'ān, prepared earlier on the order of Abū Bakr, should be published, and that publication of the Qur'ānic text in any other dialect or idiom should be proscribed.

The Qur'ān that we possess today corresponds exactly to the edition which was prepared on the orders of Abū Bakr and copies of which were officially sent, on the orders of 'Uthmān, to various cities and provinces. Several copies of this original edition of the Qur'ān still exist today. Anyone who entertains any doubt as to the authenticity of the Qur'ān can satisfy himself by obtaining a copy of the Qur'ān from any bookseller, say in West Africa, and then have a *ḥāfiẓ* (memorizer of the Qur'ān) recite it from memory, compare the two, and then compare these with the copies of the Qur'ān published through the centuries since the time of 'Uthmān. If he detects any discrepancy, even in a single letter or syllable, he should inform the whole world of his great discovery!

Not even the most sceptical person has any reason to doubt that the Qur'ān as we know it today is identical with the Qur'ān which Muḥammad (peace be on him) set before the world; this is an unquestionable, objective, historical fact, and there is nothing in human history on which the evidence is so overwhelmingly strong and conclusive. To doubt the authenticity of the Qur'ān is like doubting the existence of the Roman Empire, the Mughals of India, or Napoleon! To doubt historical facts like these is a sign of stark ignorance, not a mark of erudition and scholarship.

[VII]

The Qur'ān is a Book to which innumerable people turn for innumerable purposes. It is difficult to offer advice appropriate to all. The readers to whom this work is addressed are those who are concerned to acquire a serious understanding of the Book, and who seek the guidance it has to offer in relation to the various problems of life. For such people we have a few suggestions to make, and we shall offer some explanations in the hope of facilitating their study of the Qur'ān.

Anyone who really wishes to understand the Qur'ān, irrespective of whether or not he believes in it, must divest his mind, as far as possible, of every preconceived notion, bias and prejudice, in order to embark upon his study with an open mind. Anyone who begins to study the Qur'ān with a set of preconceived ideas is likely to read those very ideas into the Book. No book can be profitably studied with this kind of attitude, let alone the Qur'ān which refuses to open its treasure-house to such readers.

For those who want only a superficial acquaintance with the doctrines of the Qur'ān one reading is perhaps sufficient. For those who want to fathom its depths even several readings are not enough. These people need to study the Qur'ān over and over again, taking notes of everything that strikes them as significant. Those who are willing to study the Qur'ān in this manner should do so at least twice to begin with, so as to obtain a broad grasp of the system of beliefs and practical prescriptions that it offers. In this preliminary survey, they should try to gain an overall perspective of the Qur'ān and to grasp the basic ideas which it expounds, and the system of life that it seeks to build on the basis of those ideas. If, during the course of this study, anything agitates the mind of the reader, he should note down the point concerned and patiently persevere with his study. He is likely to find that, as he proceeds, the difficulties are resolved. (When a problem has been solved, it is advisable to note down the solution alongside the problem.) Experience suggests that any problems still unsolved after a first reading of the Qur'ān are likely to be resolved by a careful second reading.

Only after acquiring a total perspective of the Qur'ān should a more detailed study be attempted. Again the reader is well advised to keep noting down the various aspects of the Qur'ānic teachings. For instance, he should note the human model that the Qur'ān extols as praiseworthy, and the model it denounces. It might be helpful to make two columns, one headed 'praiseworthy qualities', the other headed 'blameworthy qualities', and then to enter into the respective columns all that is found relevant in the Qur'ān. To take another instance, the reader might proceed to investigate the Qur'ānic point of view on what is conducive to human success and felicity, as against what leads to man's ultimate failure and perdition. An efficient way to carry out this investigation would be to note under separate headings, such as 'conducive to success' and 'conducive to failure', any relevant material encountered. In the same way, the reader should take down notes about Qur'ānic teachings on questions of belief and morals, man's rights and obligations, family life and collective behaviour, economic and political life, law and social organization, war and peace, and so on. Then he should use these various teachings to try to develop an image of the Qur'ānic teachings *vis-à-vis* each particular aspect of human life. This should be followed by an attempt at integrating these images so that he comes to grasp the total scheme of life envisaged by the Qur'ān.

Moreover, anyone wishing to study in depth the Qur'ānic viewpoint on any particular problem of life should, first of all, study all the significant strands of human thought concerning that problem. Ancient and modern works on the subject should be studied. Unresolved problems where human thinking seems to have got stuck should be noted. The Qur'ān should then be studied with these unresolved problems in mind, with a view to finding out what solutions the Qur'ān has to offer. Personal experience again suggests that anyone who studies the Qur'ān in this manner will find his problem solved with the help of verses which he may have read scores of times without it ever crossing his mind that they could have any relevance to the problems at hand.

It should be remembered, nevertheless, that full appreciation of the spirit of the Qur'ān demands practical involvement with the struggle to fulfil its mission. The Qur'ān is neither a book of abstract theories and cold doctrines which the reader can grasp while seated in a cosy armchair, not is it merely a religious book like other religious books, the secrets of which can be grasped in seminaries and oratories. On the contrary, it is the blueprint and guidebook of a message, of a mission, of a movement. As soon as this Book was revealed, it drove a quiet, kind-hearted man from his isolation and seclusion, and placed him upon the battlefield of life to challenge a world that had gone astray. It inspired him to raise his voice against falsehood, and pitted him in a grim struggle against the standard-bearers of unbelief, of disobedience to God, of waywardness and error. One after the other, it sought out everyone who had a pure and noble soul, mustering them together under the standard of the Messenger. It also infuriated all those who by their nature were bent on mischief and drove them to wage war against the bearers of the Truth.

This is the Book which inspired and directed that great movement which began with the preaching of a message by an individual, and continued for no fewer than twenty-three years, until the Kingdom of God was truly established on earth. In this long and heart-rending struggle between Truth and falsehood, this Book unfailingly guided its followers to the eradication of the latter and the consolidation and enthronement of the former. How then could one expect to get to the heart of the Qur'ānic truths merely by reciting its verses, without so much as stepping upon the field of battle between faith and unbelief, between Islam and Ignorance? To appreciate the Qur'ān fully one must take it up and launch into the task of calling people to God, making it one's guide at every stage.

Then, and only then, does one meet the various experiences encountered at the time of its revelation. One experiences the initial rejection of the message of Islam by the city of Makkah, the persistent hostility leading to the quest for a haven of refuge in Abyssinia, and the attempt to win a favourable response from Ṭā'if which led, instead, to cruel persecution of the bearer of the Qur'ānic message. One experiences also the campaigns of Badr, of Uḥud, of Ḥunayn and of Tabūk. One comes face to face with Abū Jahl and Abū Lahab, with hypocrites and with Jews, with those who instantly respond to this call as well as those who, lacking clarity of perception and moral strength, were drawn into Islam only at a later stage.

This will be an experience different from any so–called 'mystic experience'. I designate it the 'Qur'ānic mystic experience'. One of the characteristics of this 'experience' is that at each stage one almost automatically finds certain Qur'ānic verses to guide one, since they were revealed at a similar stage and therefore contain the guidance appropriate to it. A person engaged in this struggle may not grasp all the linguistic and grammatical subtleties, he may also miss certain finer points in the rhetoric and semantics of the Qur'ān, yet it is impossible for the Qur'ān to fail to reveal its true spirit to him.

Again, in keeping with the same principle, a man can neither understand the laws, the moral teachings, and the economic and political principles which the Qur'ān embodies, nor appreciate the full import of the Qur'ānic laws and regulations, unless he tries to implement them in his own life. Hence the individual who fails to translate the Qur'ānic precepts into personal practice will fail to understand the Book. The same must be said of any nation that allows the institutions of its collective life to run contrary to the teachings of the Qur'ān.

[VIII]

It is well known that the Qur'ān claims to be capable of guiding all mankind. Yet the student of the Qur'ān finds that it is generally addressed to the people of Arabia, who lived in the time of its revelation. Although the Qur'ān occasionally addresses itself to all mankind its contents are, on the whole, vitally related to the taste and temperament, the environment and history, and the customs and usages of Arabia. When one notices this, one begins to question why a Book which seeks to guide all mankind to salvation should assign such importance to certain aspects of a particular people's life, and to things belonging to a particular age and clime. Failure to grasp the real cause of this may lead one to believe that the Book was originally designed to reform the Arabs of that particular age alone, and that it is only people of later times who have forced upon the Book an altogether novel interpretation, proclaiming that its aim is to guide all mankind for all time.

Some might say this with no other purpose than to vent their irrational prejudice against Islam. But leaving such people aside, a word may be said to those whose critical comments are motivated by the desire to understand things better. The latter would do well to study the Qur'ān carefully, noting down any place where they find that it has propounded either some doctrine or concept, or laid down some rule for practical conduct, relevant for the Arabs alone and exclusively conditioned by the peculiarities of a certain place or time. If, while addressing the people of a particular area at a particular period of time, attempting to refute their polytheistic beliefs and adducing arguments in support of its own doctrine of the unity of God, the Qur'ān draws upon facts with which those people were familiar, this does not warrant the conclusion that its message is relevant only for that particular people or for that particular period of time.

What ought to be considered is whether or not the Qur'ānic statements in refutation of the polytheistic beliefs of the Arabs of those days apply as well to other forms of polytheism in other parts of the world. Can the arguments advanced by the Qur'ān in that connection be used to rectify the beliefs of other polytheists? Is the Qur'ānic line of argument for establishing the unity of God, with minor adaptations, valid and persuasive for every age? If the answers are positive, there is no reason why a universal teaching should be dubbed exclusive to a particular people and age merely because it happened to be addressed originally to that people and at that particular period of time. No philosophy, ideology or doctrine consists of mere abstractions and is totally unrelated to the circumstances in which it developed. Even if such an absolute abstraction were possible it would remain confined to the scraps of paper on which it was written and would fail totally to have any impact on human life.

Moreover, if one wishes to spread any intellectual, moral and cultural movement on an international scale, it is by no means essential, in fact it is not even useful, for it to start on a global scale. If one wishes to propagate certain ideas, concepts and principles as the right bases for human life, one should begin by propagating them vigorously in the country where the message originates, and to the people whose language, temperament, customs and habits are familiar to its proponents. It will thus be possible to transform the lives of the people into a practical model of the message. Only then will it be able to attract the attention of other nations, and intelligent people living elsewhere will also try to understand it and to spread it in their own lands.

Indeed, what marks out a time-bound from an eternal, and a particularistic national doctrine from a universal one, is the fact that the former either seeks to exalt a people or claims special privileges for it or else comprises ideas and principles so vitally related to that people's life and traditions as to render it totally inapplicable to the conditions of other peoples. A universal doctrine, on the other hand, is willing to accord equal rights and status to all, and its principles have an international character in that they are equally applicable to other nations. Likewise, the validity of those doctrines which seek to come to grips merely with questions of a transient and superficial nature is time-bound. If one studies the Qur'ān with these considerations in mind, can one really conclude that it has only a particularistic national character, and that its validity is therefore time-bound?

[IX]

Those who embark upon a study of the Qur'ān often proceed with the assumption that this Book is, as it is commonly believed to be, a detailed code of guidance. However, when they actually read it, they fail to find detailed regulations regarding social, political and economic matters. In fact, they notice that the Qur'ān has not laid down detailed regulations even in respect of such oft-repeated subjects as Prayers and *Zakāh* (Purifying Alms). The reader finds this somewhat disconcerting and wonders in what sense the Qur'ān can be considered a code of guidance.

The uneasiness some people feel about this arises because they forget that God did not merely reveal a Book, but that He also designated a Prophet. Suppose some laymen were to be provided with the bare outlines of a construction plan on the understanding that they would carry out the construction as they wished. In such a case, it would be reasonable to expect that they should have very elaborate directives as to how the construction should be carried out. Suppose, however, that along with the broad outline of the plan of construction, they were also provided with a competent engineer to supervise the task. In that case, it would be quite unjustifiable to disregard the work of the engineer, on the expectation that detailed directives would form an integral part of the construction plan, and then to complain of imperfection in the plan itself. (This analogy should elucidate the position of the Prophet *vis-à-vis* the Qur'ān, for he clarified and elaborated the Qur'ān, supplementing its broad general principles by giving them precise and detailed forms, and incorporating them into practical life, his own as well as that of his followers. Tr.)

The Qur'ān, to put it succinctly, is a Book of broad general principles rather than of legal minutiae. The Book's main aim is to expound, clearly and adequately, the intellectual and moral foundations of the Islamic programme for life. It seeks to consolidate these by appealing both to man's mind and to his heart. Its method of guidance for practical Islamic life does not consist of laying down minutely detailed laws and regulations. It prefers to outline the basic framework for each aspect of human activity, and to lay down certain guidelines within which man can order his life in keeping with the Will of God. The mission of the Prophet was to give practical shape to the Islamic vision of the good life, by offering the world a model of an individual character and of a human state and society, as living embodiments of the principles of the Qur'ān.

[X]

The Qur'ān is strong in its condemnation of those who indulge in schismatic squabbling after the Book of Allah has been revealed, so causing a weakening of faith;[8] yet there has been considerable disagreement over the correct interpretations of the Qur'ānic injunctions, not only among later scholars, but even among the founders of the legal schools and the Successors.[9] Indeed, disagreement can be traced back even to the times of the Companions[10] of the Prophet. One can hardly point to a single Qur'ānic verse of legal import which has received complete unanimity as regards its interpretation. One is bound to ask whether the Qur'ānic condemnation applies to all who have disagreed in this way. If it does not, then what kind of schism and disagreement does the Qur'ān denounce?

This is quite a problem and its ramifications cannot be considered at length here. The reader may rest assured that the Qur'ān is not opposed to differences of opinion within the framework of a general agreement on the fundamentals of Islam and the broad unity of the Islamic community. In addition it is not opposed to disagreement arising from an earnest endeavour to arrive at the right conclusions on a particular subject; the only disagreements condemned by the Qur'ān are those arising out of egotism and perversity, leading to mutual strife and hostility.

The two sorts of disagreement are different in character and give rise to different results. The first kind is a stimulus to improvement and the very soul of a healthy society. Differences of this kind are found in every society whose members are endowed with intelligence and reason. Their existence is a sign of life, while their absence only serves to demonstrate that a society is not made up of intelligent men and women but of blocks of wood. Disagreements of the second kind, however, are of an altogether different character and lead to ruin and

---

8. See Qur'ān 2:7; 6:159; 42:14; 3:105; 8:46. Tr.

9. The word "Successors" has been used as the equivalent of *Tābiʿūn*, i.e. those who benefited from the Companions of the Prophet (peace be upon him). Tr.

10. The word "Companions" has been used as the equivalent of *Ṣaḥābah*, i.e. those who, in a state of belief, enjoyed the companionship of the Prophet (peace be on him). Tr.

destruction of the people among whom they arise. Far from being a sign of health, their emergence is symptomatic of a grave sickness.

The first kind of disagreement exists among scholars who are all agreed that it is their duty to obey God and His Prophet. They also agree that the Qur'ān and the *Sunnah* are their main sources of guidance. Thus, when scholarly investigation on some subsidiary question leads two or more scholars to disagree, or when two judges disagree in their judgement on some dispute, they regard neither their judgement, nor the questions on which their opinion has been expressed, as fundamentals of faith. They do not accuse those who disagree with their opinion of having left the fold of true faith. What each does is rather to proffer his arguments showing that he has done his best to investigate the matter thoroughly. It is then left to the courts (in judicial matters) and to public opinion (if the matter relates to the community at large) either to prefer whichever opinion seems the sounder, or to accept both opinions as equally permissible.

Schism occurs when the very fundamentals are made a matter of dispute and controversy. It may also happen that some scholar, mystic, *muftī*, or leader pronounces on a question to which God and His Messenger have not attached fundamental importance, exaggerating the significance of the question to such an extent that it is transformed into a basic issue of faith. Such people usually go one step further, declaring all who disagree with their opinion to have forsaken the true faith and set themselves outside the community of true believers. They may even go so far as to organize those who agree with them into a sect, claiming that sect to be identical with the Islamic community, and declaring that everyone who does not belong to it is destined to hell-fire!

Whenever the Qur'ān denounces schismatic disagreements and sectarianism, its aim is to denounce this latter kind of disagreement. As for disagreements of the first category, we encounter several examples of these even during the life of the Prophet. The Prophet not only accepted the validity of such disagreements, he even expressed approval of them. For this kind of disagreement shows that a community is not lacking in the capacity for thought, for enquiry and investigation, for

grasping or wrestling with the problems it faces. It also shows that
the intelligent members of the community are earnestly concerned
about their religion and how to apply its injunctions to the problems
of human life. It shows too that their intellectual capacities operate
within the broad framework of their religion, rather than searching
beyond its boundaries for solutions to their problems. And it proves
that the community is following the golden path of moderation. Such
moderation preserves its unity by broad agreement on fundamentals,
and at the same time provides its scholars and thinkers with full
freedom of enquiry so that they may achieve fresh insights and new
interpretations within the framework of the fundamental principles
of Islam.

[XI]

It is not intended here to survey all the questions which may arise
in the mind of a student of the Qur'ān. Many questions relate to
specific *sūrahs* or verses, and they are explained in the relevant notes.
This introduction confines itself to basic questions related to the
understanding of the Qur'ān as a whole.

The Four Primary Qur'ānic Themes

THE QUR'ĀNIC lexicon considers *ilāh*, *rabb*, *dīn* and *'ibādah* – its four primary themes – as of foundational importance to human life. Small wonder the whole focus of the Qur'ān is on Allah's centrality as *Ilāh* and *Rabb*, Who is peerless, with none to share His divinity and providence. Consistent with its emphasis on Allah's centrality, the Qur'ān asks humanity to give up everyone else and accept Allah alone as divine and providential. In this way, our whole lives fall within His realm of authority and to the exclusion of all else.

وَمَآ أَرْسَلْنَا مِن قَبْلِكَ مِن رَّسُولٍ إِلَّا نُوحِىٓ إِلَيْهِ أَنَّهُۥ لَآ إِلَٰهَ
إِلَّآ أَنَا۠ فَٱعْبُدُونِ ۞

Not a messenger did We send before you without this inspiration sent by Us to him: that there is no god but I; therefore worship and serve Me.

al-Anbiyā' 21:25

ٱتَّخَذُوٓاْ أَحْبَارَهُمْ وَرُهْبَٰنَهُمْ أَرْبَابًا مِّن دُونِ ٱللَّهِ وَٱلْمَسِيحَ ٱبْنَ مَرْيَمَ
وَمَآ أُمِرُوٓاْ إِلَّا لِيَعْبُدُوٓاْ إِلَٰهًا وَٰحِدًا لَّآ إِلَٰهَ إِلَّا هُوَ سُبْحَٰنَهُۥ
عَمَّا يُشْرِكُونَ ۞

They take their priests and their anchorites to be their lords in
derogation of Allah, and (they take as their Lord) Christ, the
son of Mary; yet they were commanded to worship but One
God: there is no god but He. Praise and glory to Him: (far is
He) from having the partners they associate (with Him).

al-Tawbah 9:31

إِنَّ هَـٰذِهِۦٓ أُمَّتُكُمْ أُمَّةً وَاحِدَةً وَأَنَا۠ رَبُّكُمْ فَٱعْبُدُونِ ۝

Verily, this brotherhood of yours is a single brotherhood,
and I am your Lord and Cherisher: therefore serve Me (and
no other).

al-Anbiyā' 21:92

قُلْ أَغَيْرَ ٱللَّهِ أَبْغِى رَبًّا وَهُوَ رَبُّ كُلِّ شَىْءٍ وَلَا تَكْسِبُ كُلُّ نَفْسٍ إِلَّا عَلَيْهَا
وَلَا تَزِرُ وَازِرَةٌ وِزْرَ أُخْرَىٰ ثُمَّ إِلَىٰ رَبِّكُم مَّرْجِعُكُمْ فَيُنَبِّئُكُم بِمَا كُنتُمْ
فِيهِ تَخْتَلِفُونَ ۝

Say: "Shall I seek for (my) Cherisher other than Allah,
when He is the Cherisher of all things (that exist)? Every
soul draws the meed of its acts on none but itself: no bearer
of burdens can bear the burden of another. Your goal in the
end is towards Allah: He will tell you the truth of the things
wherein you disputed."

al-An'ām 6:164

قُلْ إِنَّمَآ أَنَا۠ بَشَرٌ مِّثْلُكُمْ يُوحَىٰ إِلَىَّ أَنَّمَآ إِلَـٰهُكُمْ إِلَـٰهٌ وَاحِدٌ فَمَن كَانَ
يَرْجُوا۟ لِقَآءَ رَبِّهِۦ فَلْيَعْمَلْ عَمَلًا صَـٰلِحًا وَلَا يُشْرِكْ بِعِبَادَةِ رَبِّهِۦٓ أَحَدًۢا ۝

Say: "I am but a man like yourselves, (but) the inspiration
has come to me, that your God is one God: whoever expects

to meet his Lord, let him work righteousness, and, in the worship of his Lord, admit no one as partner."

al-Kahf 18:110

وَلَقَدْ بَعَثْنَا فِى كُلِّ أُمَّةٍ رَّسُولًا أَنِ ٱعْبُدُواْ ٱللَّهَ وَٱجْتَنِبُواْ ٱلطَّٰغُوتَ ۖ فَمِنْهُم مَّنْ هَدَى ٱللَّهُ وَمِنْهُم مَّنْ حَقَّتْ عَلَيْهِ ٱلضَّلَٰلَةُ ۚ فَسِيرُواْ فِى ٱلْأَرْضِ فَٱنظُرُواْ كَيْفَ كَانَ عَٰقِبَةُ ٱلْمُكَذِّبِينَ ۝

For We assuredly sent amongst every people a messenger, (with the Command), "Serve Allah, and eschew evil": of the people were some whom Allah guided, and some on whom error became inevitably (established). So travel through the earth, and see what was the end of those who denied (the Truth).

al-Naḥl 16:36

إِنَّ ٱللَّهَ رَبِّى وَرَبُّكُمْ فَٱعْبُدُوهُ ۚ هَٰذَا صِرَٰطٌ مُّسْتَقِيمٌ ۝

"It is Allah Who is my Lord and your Lord; then worship Him. This is a Way that is straight."

أَفَغَيْرَ دِينِ ٱللَّهِ يَبْغُونَ وَلَهُۥٓ أَسْلَمَ مَن فِى ٱلسَّمَٰوَٰتِ وَٱلْأَرْضِ طَوْعًا وَكَرْهًا وَإِلَيْهِ يُرْجَعُونَ ۝

Do they seek for other than the Religion of Allah? – while all creatures in the heavens and on earth have, willing or unwilling, bowed to His Will (accepted Islam), and to Him shall they all be brought back.

Āl ʿImrān 3:51, 83

These few *āyahs* are just a sample. Anyone who cares to read the Qur'ān may validate our thesis that its whole discourse revolves around these four primary themes reinforcing the centrality of the following concepts:

- Allah is the *Ilāh* and Provider.

- Divinity and providence belong to Allah alone.

- He alone should be worshipped.

- The *dīn* should be for Allah alone in intent and spirit.

- In other words, private as well as public spheres should fall under Allah's jurisdiction.

The importance of these four themes

This being the case, it is essential to grasp the instructional thrust of the Qur'ān. For if a person is neither familiar with the meaning of expressions like *ilāh* and *Rabb*, nor with the notion of *'ibādah* and *dīn*, the Qur'ān will withhold its meanings from him. In consequence, he will fail to grasp the concept of *tawḥīd* (the unicity of Allah) and its adversarial concept, *shirk* (polytheism/disbelief). With such a large failing, this person cannot surrender his affairs to Allah for guidance. Likewise, if for any reason these themes remain imprecise and obscure for readers, the Qur'ān will refuse to unfold its meaning to them. In this case even though someone may proclaim their belief in the Qur'ān, such belief and practice will be insufficient.

For instance, he may continue saying *lā ilāha illal-Lāh* – there is none but Allah – and still elevate a multitude of people and philosophies to divinity. He may also continue saying there is no master other than Allah but ascribe divinity to others as well. Again, he may say with sincerity that he worships Allah, and even then, continue worshipping a multitude of gods. He makes a full-throated proclamation of being in Allah's *dīn*, even though he allows other yokes around his neck. He may also never use the epithets of *ilāh* and *Rabb* for others, but in the matrix of these primary concepts, he still appoints to himself many *ilāh* and *Rabb*. In short, the poor soul may not have the slightest idea that he ascribes divinity and providence to humans and their manufactured icons.

Should you tell him that he is worshipping objects other than Allah and that as such, he is guilty of polytheism, he may go for your throat. Yet for sure in the parlance of worship and *dīn*, he is not Allah's but somebody else's worshipper and so is his *dīn*.

The real cause of misapprehension

Before the Qur'ān descended upon Arabia, by and large people knew the phrasal implications of *ilāh* and *Rabb* for these words were then in currency. As such, when people were told that Allah alone was their *Ilāh* and *Rabb*, that no one else shared His divinity or providence, then they got the drift of the message knowing well the inviolable nature of Allah's domain and its exclusivity. Those who opposed the call knew the implications of their refusal while those who accepted the call knew what they had to discard in their embrace of the new message. Likewise, their vocabulary carried expressions like *ʿibādah* and *dīn*. They knew what *ʿabd* entailed; what made *ʿubūdiyyah*; what attitudes were constitutive of *ʿibādah*; and what it was that *dīn* stood for. Thus when they were asked to worship none but Allah and stay away from all other forms of worship, they understood the Qur'ānic call. They knew the change it sought to bring about in their lives.

In later times, however, these words suffered from corruption and a change in meaning, which not only diluted their wider expression but also restricted them to a particular nuance. This can be attributed to declining standards in pure Arabic tastes and sensibilities. With changing times, linguistic and exegetic literature carried meanings understood by present-day Muslims. For example, the phrase *ilāh* approximated the meaning of idols and gods. *Rabb* stood for provider and sustainer. *ʿIbādah* was translated into ritualistic worship. *Dīn* became the equivalent of religion and *dharma* was transmuted into an idol or a satan. That this made the Qur'ānic intent obscure and difficult to understand soon became obvious.

The Qur'ān says do not elevate others to the status of *ilāh*. In return, people say "we have discarded idols and gods in compliance with the Qur'ānic intent," though they follow what falls within the purview of *ilāh*.

The Qur'ān also says do not accept anyone else as *Rabb*. In return, people say "for sure we have grasped the meaning of *tawḥīd* in our lives as we do not accept anyone other than Allah as our provider and sustainer," though they negate whatever the concept of *Rabb* entails by giving others the status of *Rabb*.

Likewise, the Qur'ān asks its readers to give up *ṭāghūt* and worship Allah alone. In return, they emphatically say: "we do not worship idols; we curse the satan and we submit ourselves to Allah."

Yet the fact is that other than giving up stone-crafted images, they are still deeply involved with *ṭāghūt*. And other than ritualistic worship, the object of their devotion remains anything but Allah. The same goes for *dīn*, which they have taken for a formal acceptance of a religion named Islam. "What else do you want from us," they say, "when we do not proclaim ourselves as Christians, Jews or Hindus?" Thus, anyone who is a Muslim by definition thinks his *dīn* is for Allah alone, though in the exhaustive sense of the phrase *dīn*, the majority of Muslims still lack purity in their commitment to Islam.

The consequences of this misperception

Whether we like it or not, because the meanings of these four foundational themes are veiled more than three-fourths of the Qur'ānic teachings – rather, its real spirit – has gone obscured, resulting in obvious flaws in people's beliefs and practices. To highlight the Qur'ānic nexus and elaborate its real intent, it is important that these primary concepts are fully explained. I have tried in a number of previous essays to inform people of their meanings but perhaps this has not been enough to dispel misunderstandings. Nor does it seem to have satisfied readers, for without citing the lexicon and the Qur'ānic *āyahs* in my support, people take my extrapolations as subjective. Nor can my opinion invite respect especially from those who disagree with me. My current effort, therefore, is to explain these four primary concepts fully and also avoid saying something that has no supporting evidence from the lexicon and the Qur'ān.

Ilāh: The Lexicographical Context

THE WORD *ilāh* has its roots in ا ل ه.
The words so derived are as follows:

أَلَهَ إِذَا تَحَيَّرَ

Aliha idhā taḥyyara – means: astounded and bewildered.

أَلِهْتُ إلى فُلانٍ أيْ سَكَنْتُ إلَيْه

Alihtu ilā fulān ay sakantu ilayhi – means: I felt comforted by seeking his refuge.

أَلِهَ الرَّجُلُ إِذَا فَزِعَ مِنْ أَمْرٍ نَزَلَ بِهِ فَآلَهَهُ غَيْرُهُ، أَيْ أَجَارَهُ

Alihar-rajulu idhā fazi‘a min amrin nazala bihī fa-ālahahū ghayruhū ay ajārahū – means: a person who is scared because of some calamitous event or hurt and the other gives him protection.

أَلِهَ الرَّجُلُ إلى الرَّجُلِ اتَّجَهَ إلَيْه لِشِدَّةِ شَوْقِهِ إلَيْه

Alihar-rajulu ilar-rajuli ittajaha ilayhi li-shiddati shawqihī ilayhi – means: a person who has turned towards someone else with a longing heart.

أَلَهَ الفَصِيلُ إِذَا وَلَهَ بِأُمِّهِ

Aliha'l-faṣīlu idhā waliha bi-ummihī – means: the baby camel which was separated clung to its mother when it found her.

لاَهَ يَلِيهُ لِيهاً وَلاهاً إِذَا احْتَجَبَ

Lāha yalīhu Līhan wa-lāhan idhā iḥtajaba – means: something became concealed and hidden and then raised in status.

اِلهَ اَلِهةً وَّالْوْهَةً وَّالْوْهِيَّةً عَبَدَ

Aliha ilāhatan wa ulūhatan wa ulūhiyyatan ʿabada – means: he engaged himself in worship.

One can establish from these phrases how the expressions *ilāh or ilāhatan lahū* were transfigured into worship and *ilāh* into *maʿbūd*.

1. An individual's urge to worship comes from need. He does not think of worshipping anyone unless he feels that the god he has opted for can help him realize his desires, that he can take him into his protective embrace in the face of a threatening situation or suffering, and that he can give him comfort in distress.

2. Furthermore, the concept of a relief-giver is essentially tied up with a person's belief that the former is exalted not only in stature but in power and authority as well.

3. Based on our everyday knowledge of the process involving desire and satisfaction we know that in the causal world, things or people instrumental in gratifying human needs do not generate in us the emotion of worship. For instance, a person needs money to spend; he goes to someone and asks for a job, which he is given. Now, since this whole exercise has sensory and cognitive aspects, it never generates a worship-emotion. This only comes about when the person objectified as satisfier carries a mysterious existence, when his power to deliver and his person are shrouded, inaccessible to view. Hence why in describing *maʿbūd*, the word used implies loftiness, concealment, and a surprise element.

4. The person whom one believes can help in distress or adversity is obviously someone who exerts a pull on the seeker. Inevitably, the latter turns earnestly to this person for restitution of their grievances and problems.

Thus, the use of the word *ilāh* for a god (*maʿbūd*) that deserves worship carries a whole panoply of concepts including provider, amender, protector, comforter, superior, all-powerful and exalted – someone who can spur the seeker into fulfilment and realization. Besides, he should also possess a mysterious presence, inaccessible to physical sight. Lastly, humans should feel a natural pull towards this person.

The *jāhilī* concept of *ilāh*

After tracing the roots of *ilāh* in lexicography, we now have to look into the Arabs' and the ancients' concept of *ilāh*, i.e. that which they cherished in the past, and which the Qur'ān negated.

وَٱتَّخَذُواْ مِن دُونِ ٱللَّهِ ءَالِهَةً لِّيَكُونُواْ لَهُمْ عِزًّا ۝

And they have taken (for worship) gods other than Allah, to give them power and glory!

Maryam 19:81

وَٱتَّخَذُواْ مِن دُونِ ٱللَّهِ ءَالِهَةً لَّعَلَّهُمْ يُنصَرُونَ ۝

And they have taken gods besides Allah, hoping that they will be helped.

Yā Sīn 36:74

From these two *āyahs* we now know that in people's perceptions pagan gods facilitated support and protection. They could be called upon to help people when the odds they faced were tough or detrimental, and by granting such gods their favour and attention, worshippers would be safe from fear and loss.[1]

---

1. Here are two ideas worth consideration: first, the *maʿbūd* that the *jāhilī* people really worshipped irrespective of whether he was false or true, and second, the *maʿbūd* Who deserved worship.

وَمَا ظَلَمۡنَٰهُمۡ وَلَٰكِن ظَلَمُوٓاْ أَنفُسَهُمۡ فَمَآ أَغۡنَتۡ عَنۡهُمۡ ءَالِهَتُهُمُ ٱلَّتِي
يَدۡعُونَ مِن دُونِ ٱللَّهِ مِن شَيۡءٍ لَّمَّا جَآءَ أَمۡرُ رَبِّكَ وَمَا زَادُوهُمۡ غَيۡرَ
تَتۡبِيبٍ ۝

It was not We that wronged them: they wronged their own
souls: the deities, other than Allah, whom they invoked,
profited them not at all when there issued the decree of your
Lord: nor did they add aught (to their lot) but perdition!

Hūd 11:101

وَٱلَّذِينَ يَدۡعُونَ مِن دُونِ ٱللَّهِ لَا يَخۡلُقُونَ شَيۡئًا وَهُمۡ يُخۡلَقُونَ ۝ أَمۡوَٰتٌ
غَيۡرُ أَحۡيَآءٍ وَمَا يَشۡعُرُونَ أَيَّانَ يُبۡعَثُونَ ۝ إِلَٰهُكُمۡ إِلَٰهٌ وَٰحِدٌ فَٱلَّذِينَ
لَا يُؤۡمِنُونَ بِٱلۡأَخِرَةِ قُلُوبُهُم مُّنكِرَةٌ وَهُم مُّسۡتَكۡبِرُونَ ۝

Those whom they invoke besides Allah create nothing and
are themselves created. Lifeless are they, not alive, they do
not know when they will be raised up. God of you all is the
One God. But the hearts of those who do not believe in the
Hereafter are steeped in rejection of the Truth, and they are
given to arrogance.

al-Naḥl 16:20-22

وَلَا تَدۡعُ مَعَ ٱللَّهِ إِلَٰهًا ءَاخَرَ لَآ إِلَٰهَ إِلَّا هُوَ كُلُّ شَيۡءٍ هَالِكٌ إِلَّا وَجۡهَهُۥ
لَهُ ٱلۡحُكۡمُ وَإِلَيۡهِ تُرۡجَعُونَ ۝

And call not, besides Allah, on another god. There is no god
but He. Everything (that exists) will perish except His Own
Face. To Him belongs the Command, and to Him will you
(all) be brought back.

al-Qaṣaṣ 28:88

وَمَا يَتَّبِعُ ٱلَّذِينَ يَدْعُونَ مِن دُونِ ٱللَّهِ شُرَكَآءَۚ إِن يَتَّبِعُونَ إِلَّا ٱلظَّنَّ
وَإِنْ هُمْ إِلَّا يَخْرُصُونَ ۝

What is it that they follow, who call upon associate-gods besides
Allah? They follow but a guess and are only conjecturing.

Yūnus 10:66

The preceding *āyahs* highlight certain issues. First, the *jāhilī*
people called upon their *ilāhs* to ease their difficult situations and
redeem their needs. In other words, they supplicated to them. Second,
their *ilāhs* were not only *jinn* or angels but also the dead as is evident
from "*amwātun ghayru aḥyā'in wa mā yash'urūna ayyāna yub'athūn*".
("Lifeless are they, not alive, they do not know when they will be raised
up." *Al-Naḥl* 16:21) Third, they had faith that their *ilāhs* listened to
their prayers and were capable of alleviating their distress.

To clarify the subject further, it is important to grasp the essentials
of *du'ā'* (supplication) and the help sought from the *ilāh*. For example,
if someone is thirsty and he asks his attendant for a drink, or if he falls
sick and calls for a physician, this does not fall within the purview of
du'ā'. Nor does it involve his elevating his attendant or physician to
the status of *ilāh*, for the person's action belongs to the causal world
and not to something beyond it. But if he invoked some saint or an
idol for help, then this would amount to making them an *ilāh*.

The reason for this is obvious. If a person calls out to a *walī* or
saint buried in a grave hundreds of miles away, then this amounts
to his belief in the latter's ability to hear and help him. Or it means
that he believes the saint has control over the causal world, and that
he can satisfy the needs and remove ailments. In other words, he can
supernaturally move the physical world run by causal relations. Thus,
the *ilāh* concept which in the first place gives rise to the supplicant's
prayer in the hope of being heard and redressed is essentially tied to the
notion of someone who is supernatural in his authority and power.

وَلَقَدْ أَهْلَكْنَا مَا حَوْلَكُم مِّنَ ٱلْقُرَىٰ وَصَرَّفْنَا ٱلْأَيَـٰتِ لَعَلَّهُمْ
يَرْجِعُونَ ۞ فَلَوْلَا نَصَرَهُمُ ٱلَّذِينَ ٱتَّخَذُوا۟ مِن دُونِ ٱللَّهِ قُرْبَانًا ءَالِهَةً بَلْ
ضَلُّوا۟ عَنْهُمْ وَذَٰلِكَ إِفْكُهُمْ وَمَا كَانُوا۟ يَفْتَرُونَ ۞

We destroyed aforetime populations round about you; and
We have shown the Signs in various ways, that they may turn
(to Us). Why then was no help forthcoming to them from
those whom they worshipped as gods, besides Allah, as a
means of access (to Allah)? Nay, they left them in the lurch:
but that was their falsehood and their invention.

al-Aḥqāf 46:27-28

وَمَا لِىَ لَآ أَعْبُدُ ٱلَّذِى فَطَرَنِى وَإِلَيْهِ تُرْجَعُونَ ۞ ءَأَتَّخِذُ مِن دُونِهِ ءَالِهَةً
إِن يُرِدْنِ ٱلرَّحْمَـٰنُ بِضُرٍّ لَّا تُغْنِ عَنِّى شَفَـٰعَتُهُمْ شَيْـًٔا وَلَا يُنقِذُونِ ۞

It would not be reasonable for me if I did not serve Him Who
created me, and to Whom you shall (all) be brought back. Shall
I take (other) gods besides Him? If (Allah) most Gracious
should intend some adversity for me, of no use whatever will
be their intercession for me, nor can they deliver me.

Yā Sīn 36:22-23

أَلَا لِلَّهِ ٱلدِّينُ ٱلْخَالِصُ وَٱلَّذِينَ ٱتَّخَذُوا۟ مِن دُونِهِ أَوْلِيَآءَ مَا نَعْبُدُهُمْ
إِلَّا لِيُقَرِّبُونَآ إِلَى ٱللَّهِ زُلْفَىٰ إِنَّ ٱللَّهَ يَحْكُمُ بَيْنَهُمْ فِى مَا هُمْ فِيهِ يَخْتَلِفُونَ إِنَّ
ٱللَّهَ لَا يَهْدِى مَنْ هُوَ كَـٰذِبٌ كَفَّارٌ ۞

Is it not to Allah that sincere devotion is due? But those who
take for protectors others than Allah (say): "We only serve
them in order that they may bring us nearer to Allah." Truly
Allah will judge between them in that wherein they differ.
But Allah guides not such as are false and ungrateful.

al-Zumar 39:3

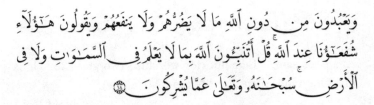

They serve, besides Allah, things that hurt them not nor profit them, and they say: "These are our intercessors with Allah." Say: "Do you indeed inform Allah of something He knows not, in the heavens or on earth? – Glory to Him! And far is He above the partners they ascribe (to Him)!"

Yūnus 10:18

These *āyahs* amplify additional aspects which tell us that the *jāhilī* people did not consider their pantheon of gods as the sole holders of divine powers. Nor did they think that there was no superior God to their pantheon of gods. In fact, they had a clear notion of a higher God, and for whom they used the word Allah.

The other gods, they believed, enjoyed some clout with this higher God, which they could use to their advantage and, thus, stay out of harm's way. Based on such notions, *jāhilī* people exalted their gods to the status of the *ilāh* reserved for Allah alone. According to their terminology, ascribing intercessory powers to someone or thing and seeking their or its help by means of a variety of rituals – whether submissive, sacrificial or charitable – divinized that person or thing as an *ilāh*.[2]

---

2. This calls for clarification. Intercession is of two kinds. The first supposedly stems from some kind of power and influence, which is used and made to prevail. The second kind is only a request – a plea that may or may not be accepted. There is no compulsive influence behind it. In the first sense, taking someone as an intercessory means that he has been upgraded to *ilāh* – a partner with Allah. The Qur'ān repudiates this kind of intercession. In the second sense, all prophets, angels, the pious among the Muslim *ummah*, and other Muslims can intercede for others. Allah has the discretion to accept or reject their intercession. The Qur'ān affirms this.

وَقَالَ ٱللَّهُ لَا تَتَّخِذُوٓاْ إِلَٰهَيْنِ ٱثْنَيْنِ ۖ إِنَّمَا هُوَ إِلَٰهٌ وَٰحِدٌ ۖ فَإِيَّٰىَ فَٱرْهَبُونِ ۝

Allah has said: "Take not (for worship) two gods: for He is just One God: then fear Me (and Me alone)."

al-Naḥl 16:51

وَحَآجَّهُۥ قَوْمُهُۥ ۚ قَالَ أَتُحَٰجُّوٓنِّى فِى ٱللَّهِ وَقَدْ هَدَىٰنِ ۚ وَلَآ أَخَافُ مَا تُشْرِكُونَ بِهِۦٓ إِلَّآ أَن يَشَآءَ رَبِّى شَيْـًٔا ۚ وَسِعَ رَبِّى كُلَّ شَىْءٍ عِلْمًا ۗ أَفَلَا تَتَذَكَّرُونَ ۝

His people disputed with him. He said: "(Come) you to dispute with me, about Allah, when He (Himself) has guided me? I fear not (the beings) you associate with Allah: unless my Lord wills, (nothing can happen). My Lord comprehends in His knowledge all things. Will you not (yourselves) be admonished?"

al-Anʿām 6:80

إِن نَّقُولُ إِلَّا ٱعْتَرَىٰكَ بَعْضُ ءَالِهَتِنَا بِسُوٓءٍ ۗ قَالَ إِنِّىٓ أُشْهِدُ ٱللَّهَ وَٱشْهَدُوٓاْ أَنِّى بَرِىٓءٌ مِّمَّا تُشْرِكُونَ ۝

"We say nothing but that (perhaps) some of our gods may have seized you with imbecility." He said: "I call Allah to witness, and do you bear witness, that I am free from the sin of ascribing, to Him."

Hūd 11:54

The *āyahs* cited above throw further light on the *jāhilī* people's attitudes towards making *ilāh* out of human material. Annoying their *ilāh*, they thought, would invite sickness, famine and other harm to their persons and belongings.

ٱتَّخَذُوٓاْ أَحْبَارَهُمْ وَرُهْبَـٰنَهُمْ أَرْبَابًا مِّن دُونِ ٱللَّهِ وَٱلْمَسِيحَ ٱبْنَ مَرْيَمَ وَمَآ أُمِرُوٓاْ إِلَّا لِيَعْبُدُوٓاْ إِلَـٰهًا وَٰحِدًا لَّآ إِلَـٰهَ إِلَّا هُوَ سُبْحَـٰنَهُۥ عَمَّا يُشْرِكُونَ ۝

They take their priests and their anchorites to be their lords in derogation of Allah, and (they take as their Lord) Christ, the son of Mary; yet they were commanded to worship but One God: there is no god but He. Praise and glory to Him: (far is He) from having the partners they associate (with Him).

al-Tawbah 9:31

أَرَءَيْتَ مَنِ ٱتَّخَذَ إِلَـٰهَهُۥ هَوَىٰهُ أَفَأَنتَ تَكُونُ عَلَيْهِ وَكِيلًا ۝

Have you seen him who takes for his god his own passion (or impulse)? Would you be a disposer of affairs for him?

al-Furqān 25:43

وَكَذَٰلِكَ زَيَّنَ لِكَثِيرٍ مِّنَ ٱلْمُشْرِكِينَ قَتْلَ أَوْلَـٰدِهِمْ شُرَكَآؤُهُمْ لِيُرْدُوهُمْ وَلِيَلْبِسُواْ عَلَيْهِمْ دِينَهُمْ وَلَوْ شَآءَ ٱللَّهُ مَا فَعَلُوهُ فَذَرْهُمْ وَمَا يَفْتَرُونَ ۝

Even so, in the eyes of most of the Pagans, their "partners" made alluring the slaughter of their children, in order to lead them to their own destruction, and cause confusion in their religion. If Allah had willed, they would not have done so: but leave them alone and their inventions.

al-Anʿām 6:137

أَمْ لَهُمْ شُرَكَـٰٓؤُاْ شَرَعُواْ لَهُم مِّنَ ٱلدِّينِ مَا لَمْ يَأْذَنۢ بِهِ ٱللَّهُ وَلَوْلَا كَلِمَةُ ٱلْفَصْلِ لَقُضِىَ بَيْنَهُمْ وَإِنَّ ٱلظَّـٰلِمِينَ لَهُمْ عَذَابٌ أَلِيمٌ ۝

Have they associate-gods who have instituted for them a religion which Allah has not approved?

al-Shūrā 42:21

These *āyahs* provide a new aspect to the word *ilāh*, different from the meanings revealed so far. Here, there is no element of supernatural sovereignty; instead, the one raised as an *ilāh* is a human being, whether this be another person or one's own self. This *ilāh* is not the kind to whom one can return for the dispensation of benefits and harm or whose protection is sought from fears and threats. He has been crafted into an *ilāh* because his wish has the force of law; his edicts are followed; his standards of *halāl* and *harām* enjoy acceptance. In other words, it has been presumed that he has the authority to issue laws and proscribe things, and that there is no other power higher than him for reference and authorization.

Here, it is of special significance to note that in the first *āyah* there is a reference about turning religious scholars and monks into *ilāh*. A *hadīth* explains this. When 'Adī ibn Hātim asked the Prophet (*'alayhis-salām*) about this *āyah*, he said people elevated their *'ulamā'* and monks as the sole determinants of that which is *halāl* and *harām*, which they respected regardless of Allah's say on the subject.

As for the second *āyah*, its meaning is transparent: a person who listens to the cadence of his own self and considers its bidding superior to the *Sharī'ah*, elevates his own self to the rank of *ilāh*.

In the last two *āyahs* quoted above though the substitute word *shurakā'* is used, the thematic thrust is the same – that is, people have exalted and divinized certain individuals and things as *ilāhs*. The two *āyahs* clearly state their view on the subject – namely, that those who follow human-made *ilāhs* and human laws in defiance of Allah's guidance are guilty of equating the earthly lawgiver with God.

Common factors in the *ilāh* concept

The meanings so far stated about *ilāh* share a common and logical thread. Anyone who visualizes someone else as supernatural, and who then considers this person as his supporter and helper, the redeemer of his difficulties and problems, the respondent of his prayers, the dispenser of his profit and loss, does so because he believes this *ilāh* has a share in the dominative control of the universe. Likewise, someone who is scared and makes a corresponding change in his behaviour based on the hurt or profit potential that he thinks an individual he visualizes as supernatural can perform is nothing but *shirk* (polytheism) for it originates from his belief that this *ilāh* has a share in the power that controls the universe. In the same vein, someone who believes in one superior God but goes to others for relief has the same god complex because he too considers his visualized supernatural man-god as having a share in divinity. Furthermore, someone who takes someone else's decree as binding is equally guilty of accepting that individual as sovereign. The real essence of Godhead is power and control. Whether this dominative power is perceived as supernatural or human, the *ilāh* concept nonetheless remains power-based.

The Qur'ānic rationale

It is this power concept which serves as the basis for the Qur'ān's emphatic negation of all non-Allah based divinity, and similarly its equally emphatic affirmation that Allah is the sole God. Its rationale lies in the fact that in the heavens and the earth there is only One Being Who has absolute power and authority: creation belongs to Him, as do beneficence and command. Everything is bonded into His obedience since He is the fount of all power. None knows the secrets of creation and its management but Him. In fact, there is no *ilāh* other than Him. That being the case, everything that a person pursues for a fictitious *ilāh* whether it is of a supplicatory nature or by way of seeking protection, or out of fear and hope, or of an intercessory nature, or of admitting someone as the originator of a command and then following him, is altogether wrong. The whole phalanx of relationships that one builds for a false *ilāh* should have been for Allah only, for He alone has power and the means of governance. One can see this Qur'ānic rationale in the following *āyahs*:

وَهُوَ ٱلَّذِى فِى ٱلسَّمَآءِ إِلَٰهٌ وَفِى ٱلْأَرْضِ إِلَٰهٌ وَهُوَ ٱلْحَكِيمُ ٱلْعَلِيمُ ۝

It is He Who is God in heaven and God on earth: and He is full of wisdom and knowledge.

al-Zukhruf 43:84

أَفَمَن يَخْلُقُ كَمَن لَّا يَخْلُقُ أَفَلَا تَذَكَّرُونَ ۝ وَإِن تَعُدُّواْ نِعْمَةَ ٱللَّهِ
لَا تُحْصُوهَآ إِنَّ ٱللَّهَ لَغَفُورٌ رَّحِيمٌ ۝ وَٱللَّهُ يَعْلَمُ مَا تُسِرُّونَ وَمَا تُعْلِنُونَ ۝
وَٱلَّذِينَ يَدْعُونَ مِن دُونِ ٱللَّهِ لَا يَخْلُقُونَ شَيْئًا وَهُمْ يُخْلَقُونَ ۝ أَمْوَاتٌ
غَيْرُ أَحْيَآءٍ وَمَا يَشْعُرُونَ أَيَّانَ يُبْعَثُونَ ۝ إِلَـٰهُكُمْ إِلَـٰهٌ وَاحِدٌ فَٱلَّذِينَ
لَا يُؤْمِنُونَ بِٱلْآخِرَةِ قُلُوبُهُم مُّنكِرَةٌ وَهُم مُّسْتَكْبِرُونَ ۝

Is then He Who creates like one that creates not? Will you
not receive admonition? If you would count up the favours
of Allah, never would you be able to number them; for Allah
is Oft-Forgiving, Most Merciful. And Allah does know what
you conceal, and what you reveal. Those whom they invoke
besides Allah create nothing and are themselves created.
(They are things) dead, lifeless: nor do they know when they
will be raised up. Your God is One God: as to those who
believe not in the Hereafter, their hearts refuse to know, and
they are arrogant.

al-Naḥl 16:17-22

يَـٰٓأَيُّهَا ٱلنَّاسُ ٱذْكُرُواْ نِعْمَتَ ٱللَّهِ عَلَيْكُمْ هَلْ مِنْ خَـٰلِقٍ غَيْرُ ٱللَّهِ
يَرْزُقُكُم مِّنَ ٱلسَّمَآءِ وَٱلْأَرْضِ لَآ إِلَـٰهَ إِلَّا هُوَ فَأَنَّىٰ تُؤْفَكُونَ ۝

O men! Call to mind the grace of Allah unto you! Is there a
Creator, other than Allah, to give you sustenance from heaven
or earth? There is no god but He: how then are you deluded
away from the Truth?

Fāṭir 35:3

قُلْ أَرَءَيْتُمْ إِنْ أَخَذَ ٱللَّهُ سَمْعَكُمْ وَأَبْصَـٰرَكُمْ وَخَتَمَ عَلَىٰ قُلُوبِكُم مَّنْ إِلَـٰهٌ
غَيْرُ ٱللَّهِ يَأْتِيكُم بِهِ ٱنظُرْ كَيْفَ نُصَرِّفُ ٱلْآيَـٰتِ ثُمَّ هُمْ يَصْدِفُونَ ۝

Say: "Do you think if Allah took away your hearing and your sight, and sealed up your hearts, who – a god other than Allah – could restore them to you? See how We explain the signs by various (symbols); yet they turn aside."

al-Anʿām 6:46

وَهُوَ ٱللَّهُ لَآ إِلَـٰهَ إِلَّا هُوَ لَهُ ٱلْحَمْدُ فِى ٱلْأُولَىٰ وَٱلْأَخِرَةِ وَلَهُ ٱلْحُكْمُ وَإِلَيْهِ تُرْجَعُونَ ۝ قُلْ أَرَءَيْتُمْ إِن جَعَلَ ٱللَّهُ عَلَيْكُمُ ٱلَّيْلَ سَرْمَدًا إِلَىٰ يَوْمِ ٱلْقِيَـٰمَةِ مَنْ إِلَـٰهٌ غَيْرُ ٱللَّهِ يَأْتِيكُم بِضِيَاءٍ أَفَلَا تَسْمَعُونَ ۝ قُلْ أَرَءَيْتُمْ إِن جَعَلَ ٱللَّهُ عَلَيْكُمُ ٱلنَّهَارَ سَرْمَدًا إِلَىٰ يَوْمِ ٱلْقِيَـٰمَةِ مَنْ إِلَـٰهٌ غَيْرُ ٱللَّهِ يَأْتِيكُم بِلَيْلٍ تَسْكُنُونَ فِيهِ أَفَلَا تُبْصِرُونَ ۝

And He is Allah: there is no god but He. To Him be praise, at the first and at the last: for Him is the command, and to Him shall you (all) be brought back. Say: Think! If Allah were to make the night perpetual over you to the Day of Judgement, what god is there other than Allah, who can give you enlightenment? Will you not then listen? Say: Think! If Allah were to make the day perpetual over you to the Day of Judgement, what god is there other than Allah, who can give you a night in which you can rest? Will you not then see?

al-Qaṣaṣ 28:70–72

قُلِ ٱدْعُواْ ٱلَّذِينَ زَعَمْتُم مِّن دُونِ ٱللَّهِ لَا يَمْلِكُونَ مِثْقَالَ ذَرَّةٍ فِى ٱلسَّمَـٰوَٰتِ وَلَا فِى ٱلْأَرْضِ وَمَا لَهُمْ فِيهِمَا مِن شِرْكٍ وَمَا لَهُۥ مِنْهُم مِّن ظَهِيرٍ ۝ وَلَا تَنفَعُ ٱلشَّفَـٰعَةُ عِندَهُۥٓ إِلَّا لِمَنْ أَذِنَ لَهُۥ حَتَّىٰٓ إِذَا فُزِّعَ عَن قُلُوبِهِمْ قَالُواْ مَاذَا قَالَ رَبُّكُمْ قَالُواْ ٱلْحَقَّ وَهُوَ ٱلْعَلِىُّ ٱلْكَبِيرُ ۝

Say: "Call upon other (gods) whom you fancy besides Allah: they have no power – not the weight of an atom – in the heavens or on earth: no (sort of) share have they therein, nor is any of them a helper to Allah. No intercession can avail in His presence, except for those for whom He has granted permission. So far (is this the case) that, when terror is removed from their hearts (at the Day of Judgement, then) will they say, 'What is it that your Lord commanded?' They will say: 'That which is true and just; and He is the Most High, Most Great.'"

Saba' 34:22-23

خَلَقَ ٱلسَّمَـٰوَٰتِ وَٱلْأَرْضَ بِٱلْحَقِّ يُكَوِّرُ ٱلَّيْلَ عَلَى ٱلنَّهَارِ وَيُكَوِّرُ ٱلنَّهَارَ عَلَى ٱلَّيْلِ وَسَخَّرَ ٱلشَّمْسَ وَٱلْقَمَرَ كُلٌّ يَجْرِى لِأَجَلٍ مُّسَمًّى أَلَا هُوَ ٱلْعَزِيزُ ٱلْغَفَّـٰرُ ۞ خَلَقَكُم مِّن نَّفْسٍ وَٰحِدَةٍ ثُمَّ جَعَلَ مِنْهَا زَوْجَهَا وَأَنزَلَ لَكُم مِّنَ ٱلْأَنْعَـٰمِ ثَمَـٰنِيَةَ أَزْوَٰجٍ يَخْلُقُكُمْ فِى بُطُونِ أُمَّهَـٰتِكُمْ خَلْقًا مِّنْ بَعْدِ خَلْقٍ فِى ظُلُمَـٰتٍ ثَلَـٰثٍ ذَٰلِكُمُ ٱللَّهُ رَبُّكُمْ لَهُ ٱلْمُلْكُ لَآ إِلَـٰهَ إِلَّا هُوَ فَأَنَّىٰ تُصْرَفُونَ ۞

He created the heavens and the earth in true (proportions): He makes the night overlap the day, and the day overlap the night: He has subjected the sun and the moon (to His law): each one follows a course for a time appointed. Is not He the Exalted in power – He Who forgives again and again? He created you (all) from a single person: then created, of like nature, his mate: and He sent down for you eight head of cattle in pairs: He makes you, in the wombs of your mothers, in stages, one after another, in three veils of darkness. Such is Allah, your Lord and Cherisher: to Him belongs (all) dominion. There is no god but He: then how are you turned away (from your true Centre)?

al-Zumar 39:5-6

أَمَّنْ خَلَقَ ٱلسَّمَـٰوَٰتِ وَٱلْأَرْضَ وَأَنزَلَ لَكُم مِّنَ ٱلسَّمَآءِ مَآءً فَأَنۢبَتْنَا بِهِۦ
حَدَآئِقَ ذَاتَ بَهْجَةٍ مَّا كَانَ لَكُمْ أَن تُنۢبِتُواْ شَجَرَهَآ أَءِلَـٰهٌ مَّعَ ٱللَّهِ بَلْ
هُمْ قَوْمٌ يَعْدِلُونَ ۝ أَمَّن جَعَلَ ٱلْأَرْضَ قَرَارًا وَجَعَلَ خِلَـٰلَهَآ أَنْهَـٰرًا
وَجَعَلَ لَهَا رَوَٰسِىَ وَجَعَلَ بَيْنَ ٱلْبَحْرَيْنِ حَاجِزًا أَءِلَـٰهٌ مَّعَ ٱللَّهِ بَلْ
أَكْثَرُهُمْ لَا يَعْلَمُونَ ۝ أَمَّن يُجِيبُ ٱلْمُضْطَرَّ إِذَا دَعَاهُ وَيَكْشِفُ ٱلسُّوٓءَ
وَيَجْعَلُكُمْ خُلَفَآءَ ٱلْأَرْضِ أَءِلَـٰهٌ مَّعَ ٱللَّهِ قَلِيلًا مَّا تَذَكَّرُونَ ۝ أَمَّن
يَهْدِيكُمْ فِى ظُلُمَـٰتِ ٱلْبَرِّ وَٱلْبَحْرِ وَمَن يُرْسِلُ ٱلرِّيَـٰحَ بُشْرًۢا بَيْنَ يَدَىْ
رَحْمَتِهِۦ أَءِلَـٰهٌ مَّعَ ٱللَّهِ تَعَـٰلَى ٱللَّهُ عَمَّا يُشْرِكُونَ ۝ أَمَّن يَبْدَؤُاْ ٱلْخَلْقَ ثُمَّ
يُعِيدُهُۥ وَمَن يَرْزُقُكُم مِّنَ ٱلسَّمَآءِ وَٱلْأَرْضِ أَءِلَـٰهٌ مَّعَ ٱللَّهِ قُلْ هَاتُواْ
بُرْهَـٰنَكُمْ إِن كُنتُمْ صَـٰدِقِينَ ۝

Or, Who has created the heavens and the earth, and Who sends you down rain from the sky? We cause to grow well-planted orchards full of beauty and delight: it is not in your power to cause the growth of the trees in them. (Can there be another) god besides Allah? Nay, they are a people who swerve from justice. Or, Who has made the earth firm to live in; made rivers in its midst; set thereon mountains immovable, and made a separating bar between the two bodies of flowing water? (Can there be another) god besides Allah? Nay, most of them know not. Or, Who listens to the (soul) distressed when it calls on Him, and Who relieves its suffering, and makes you (mankind, inheritors of the earth? (Can there be another) god besides Allah? Little it is that you heed! Or, Who guides you through the depths of darkness on land and sea, and Who sends the winds as heralds of glad tidings, going before His mercy? (Can there be another) god besides Allah? – High is Allah above what they associate with

Him! Or, Who originates creation, then repeats it, and Who gives you sustenance from heaven and earth? (Can there be another) god besides Allah? Say, "Bring forth your argument, if you are telling the truth!"

al-Naml 27:60-64

ٱلَّذِى لَهُۥ مُلْكُ ٱلسَّمَـٰوَٰتِ وَٱلْأَرْضِ وَلَمْ يَتَّخِذْ وَلَدًا وَلَمْ يَكُن لَّهُۥ شَرِيكٌ فِى ٱلْمُلْكِ وَخَلَقَ كُلَّ شَىْءٍ فَقَدَّرَهُۥ تَقْدِيرًا ۞ وَٱتَّخَذُوا۟ مِن دُونِهِۦٓ ءَالِهَةً لَّا يَخْلُقُونَ شَيْـًٔا وَهُمْ يُخْلَقُونَ وَلَا يَمْلِكُونَ لِأَنفُسِهِمْ ضَرًّا وَلَا نَفْعًا وَلَا يَمْلِكُونَ مَوْتًا وَلَا حَيَوٰةً وَلَا نُشُورًا ۞

He to Whom belongs the dominion of the heavens and the earth: no son has He begotten, nor has He a partner in His dominion: it is He Who created all things, and ordered them in due proportions. Yet they have taken, besides Him, gods that can create nothing but are themselves created; that have no control of hurt or good to themselves; nor can they control death nor life nor Resurrection.

al-Furqān 25:2-3

بَدِيعُ ٱلسَّمَـٰوَٰتِ وَٱلْأَرْضِ أَنَّىٰ يَكُونُ لَهُۥ وَلَدٌ وَلَمْ تَكُن لَّهُۥ صَـٰحِبَةٌ وَخَلَقَ كُلَّ شَىْءٍ وَهُوَ بِكُلِّ شَىْءٍ عَلِيمٌ ۞ ذَٰلِكُمُ ٱللَّهُ رَبُّكُمْ لَآ إِلَـٰهَ إِلَّا هُوَ خَـٰلِقُ كُلِّ شَىْءٍ فَٱعْبُدُوهُ وَهُوَ عَلَىٰ كُلِّ شَىْءٍ وَكِيلٌ ۞

To Him is due the primal origin of the heavens and the earth: how can He have a son when He has no consort? He created all things, and He has full knowledge of all things. That is Allah, your Lord! There is no god but He, the Creator of all things; then worship you Him; and He has power to dispose of all affairs.

al-An'ām 6:101-102

وَمِنَ ٱلنَّاسِ مَن يَتَّخِذُ مِن دُونِ ٱللَّهِ أَندَادًا يُحِبُّونَهُمْ كَحُبِّ ٱللَّهِ وَٱلَّذِينَ
ءَامَنُوٓاْ أَشَدُّ حُبًّا لِّلَّهِ وَلَوْ يَرَى ٱلَّذِينَ ظَلَمُوٓاْ إِذْ يَرَوْنَ ٱلْعَذَابَ أَنَّ ٱلْقُوَّةَ لِلَّهِ
جَمِيعًا وَأَنَّ ٱللَّهَ شَدِيدُ ٱلْعَذَابِ ۝

Yet there are men who take (for worship) others besides
Allah, as equal (with Allah): they love them as they should
love Allah. But those of faith are overflowing in their love for
Allah. If only the unrighteous could see, behold, they would
see the penalty: that to Allah belongs all power, and Allah will
strongly enforce the penalty.

al-Baqarah 2:165

قُلْ أَرَءَيْتُم مَّا تَدْعُونَ مِن دُونِ ٱللَّهِ أَرُونِى مَاذَا خَلَقُواْ مِنَ ٱلْأَرْضِ أَمْ لَهُمْ
شِرْكٌ فِى ٱلسَّمَٰوَٰتِ ٱئْتُونِى بِكِتَٰبٍ مِّن قَبْلِ هَٰذَآ أَوْ أَثَٰرَةٍ مِّنْ عِلْمٍ إِن
كُنتُمْ صَٰدِقِينَ ۝ وَمَنْ أَضَلُّ مِمَّن يَدْعُواْ مِن دُونِ ٱللَّهِ مَن لَّا يَسْتَجِيبُ
لَهُۥٓ إِلَىٰ يَوْمِ ٱلْقِيَٰمَةِ وَهُمْ عَن دُعَآئِهِمْ غَٰفِلُونَ ۝

Say: "Do you see what it is you invoke besides Allah? Show
me what it is they have created on earth, or have they a share
in the heavens? Bring me a Book (revealed) before this, or any
remnant of knowledge (you may have), if you are telling the
truth! And who is more astray than one who invokes besides
Allah, such as will not answer him on the Day of Judgement,
and who (in fact) are unconscious of their call (to them)."

al-Aḥqāf 46:4-5

لَوْ كَانَ فِيهِمَآ ءَالِهَةٌ إِلَّا ٱللَّهُ لَفَسَدَتَا فَسُبْحَٰنَ ٱللَّهِ رَبِّ ٱلْعَرْشِ
عَمَّا يَصِفُونَ ۝ لَا يُسْـَٔلُ عَمَّا يَفْعَلُ وَهُمْ يُسْـَٔلُونَ ۝

If there were, in the heavens and the earth, other gods besides
Allah, there would have been confusion in both! But glory

to Allah, the Lord of the Throne: (High is He) above what
they attribute to Him! He cannot be questioned for His acts,
but they will be questioned (for theirs).

al-Anbiyā' 21:22-23

مَا ٱتَّخَذَ ٱللَّهُ مِن وَلَدٍ وَمَا كَانَ مَعَهُۥ مِنْ إِلَـٰهٍ إِذًا لَّذَهَبَ كُلُّ إِلَـٰهٍ بِمَا خَلَقَ
وَلَعَلَا بَعْضُهُمْ عَلَىٰ بَعْضٍ سُبْحَـٰنَ ٱللَّهِ عَمَّا يَصِفُونَ ۝

No son did Allah beget, nor is there any god along with Him:
(if there were many gods), behold, each god would have taken
away what he had created, and some would have lorded it over
others! Glory to Allah! (He is free) from the (sort of) things
they attribute to Him!

al-Mu'minūn 23:91

قُل لَّوۡ كَانَ مَعَهُۥٓ ءَالِهَةٌ كَمَا يَقُولُونَ إِذًا لَّٱبْتَغَوۡاْ إِلَىٰ ذِى ٱلْعَرْشِ سَبِيلًا ۝
سُبْحَـٰنَهُۥ وَتَعَـٰلَىٰ عَمَّا يَقُولُونَ عُلُوًّا كَبِيرًا ۝

Say: "If there had been (other) gods with Him – as they say
– behold, they would certainly have sought out a way to the
Lord of the Throne! Glory to Him! He is high above all that
they say! – Exalted and Great (beyond measure)."

al-Isrā' 17:42-43

These *āyahs* centre on the notion that divinity, power, and
domination are coterminous. By their essence and meaning they are
the same things. He who lacks transcendence cannot be *ilāh*, nor should
he ever entertain its notion. Common sense and logic demand that
divinity should belong to someone who wields control and dominance.
For whatever humanity needs from an *ilāh* or whatever the material
and emotional compulsions that pushed humanity to search for an
ilāh can only be met by someone who has the dominative power to
deliver and satisfy.

What this means is that any aspiration for divinity by a non-sovereign element or a search for its presence in pitilessly incomplete creatures is pathetically inconsequential. Sooner or later, reality will demonstrate where the real divinity lays.

This being the core Qur'ānic belief, its postulates and implications can be well understood in the following ways.

First, the ability to solve problems, to give protection against all odds, to grant beneficence, to provide security and support in distress, which in our naivety we think as normal run of the mill achievements, are in fact no small matters. These are linked with the whole system of creation and management of the universe. Reflect, for example, on how even the smallest of our needs are fulfilled, and then know that without the cumulative movement of innumerable causative elements in the grand universal machine, their maturation would not have been possible.

Allah knows how much effort goes into the sun, earth, winds and seas synchronizing to produce just an ordinary glass of water or a small grain of wheat. So to hear our prayers and respond to them requires the presence of someone uncommonly powerful, someone who has created the universe, pushed the planets into orbital motions, circulated the winds and made the rain fall. In short, only He has the genius to run every part of this immense cosmology.

Second, by sheer logic, this power must be indivisible. For it is an impossible proposition for creative power to be vested in one individual while the task of feeding humanity rests with someone else. Likewise, what if the sun was owned by one person, and the earth by someone else? Furthermore, what if the power to procreate was exercised by one individual, and the power to heal by another, while matters of life and death were anchored in a third person. If this were the case, surely logic dictates that the system would grind to a halt. What this means, therefore, is that the central command's indivisibility and its power nexus is an unassailable truth for it is cognate with efficient system management. At the same time, this unitary profile of divine power calls for our respect, not least because the universe is run by this single Master.

Third, when all powers are wielded by one Sovereign Master and none other, then divinity is also exclusive to Him. After all, Who else has the power to alleviate our discomfort, concede our prayers, give us protection, and dispense good or withhold harm from us other than Him? Thus, no matter what context in which we place our *ilāh* none qualifies for this exalted spot but Him. In fact, no one could claim himself an *ilāh* even in the sense of being influential with this Universal Sovereign – no one has the ability to make Him change His decisions or alter the way the planetary system runs. To accept or not accept any plea we make falls within the ambit of His privilege and discretion.

Fourth, consistent with this uniaxial notion of sovereignty, all kinds of governance should rest with one sovereign; not even a fraction belongs to anyone else. Since He is the Creator of everything He has fashioned, then those who owe their existence to Him cannot make the absurd claim of sharing His divinity. Likewise, when He is the sole dispenser of sustenance and support to all kinds of life, those who receive His beneficence cannot have a share in His attributes or in His prerogative and power to run existence. All things considered then He alone should be the Sovereign and the Lawgiver. Indeed, one can even go so far as to say that any claim to governance and lawmaking beyond His is equally absurd. Logic does not support such a claim. Likewise, since creativity and sustenance, birth and death, control over the sun and the moon, the day-and-night cycle, decision making and determination, dominion and command and its explication are aspects of a totalizing power, people who abide by any decree issued by someone other than Allah are guilty of *shirk*. Indeed, this is similar to the *shirk* committed by one who prays to any but Allah.

Furthermore, if someone arrogates to himself the custodial ownership of a nation, sovereignty, and governance, then this is similar to his claim to divinity in a metaphysical sense, i.e. of being a patron, a redeemer, and a protector. Hence why, in the Qur'ānic lexicon of divinity, Allah is not only the sole possessor of the powers to create, cause decay and run the universe, He is also the only Lawgiver. For example, the Qur'ān says "*lahū al-ḥukm*" (His is the command) and "*lahū al-mulk*" (His is the power) as well as "*lam yakun lahū sharīkun fī al-mulk*" (There is no partner with Him in power) which clearly means that in the sense of *ulūhīyah* (divinity), sovereignty and dominion are equally entailed. For it is important for the unitarian concept of the *Ilāh* that none must be stringed with Him in His powers. Expounding on this subject, the Qur'ān says:

$$\text{قُلِ ٱللَّهُمَّ مَـٰلِكَ ٱلْمُلْكِ تُؤْتِى ٱلْمُلْكَ مَن تَشَآءُ وَتَنزِعُ ٱلْمُلْكَ مِمَّن تَشَآءُ}$$
$$\text{وَتُعِزُّ مَن تَشَآءُ وَتُذِلُّ مَن تَشَآءُ بِيَدِكَ ٱلْخَيْرُ إِنَّكَ عَلَىٰ كُلِّ شَىْءٍ قَدِيرٌ ۝}$$

Say: "O Allah! Lord of Power (and Rule), You give power to whom You please, and You strip off power from whom You please: You endue with honour whom You please, and You bring low whom You please: in Your hand is all good. Verily, over all things You have power."

Āl ʿImrān 3:26

$$\text{فَتَعَـٰلَى ٱللَّهُ ٱلْمَلِكُ ٱلْحَقُّ لَآ إِلَـٰهَ إِلَّا هُوَ رَبُّ ٱلْعَرْشِ ٱلْكَرِيمِ ۝}$$

Therefore exalted be Allah, the King, the Reality: there is no god but He, the Lord of the Throne of Honour!

al-Muʾminūn 23:116

$$\text{قُلْ أَعُوذُ بِرَبِّ ٱلنَّاسِ ۝ مَلِكِ ٱلنَّاسِ ۝ إِلَـٰهِ ٱلنَّاسِ ۝}$$

Say: I seek refuge with the Lord and Cherisher of mankind, the King (or Ruler) of mankind, the God (or Judge) of mankind.

al-Nās 114:1-3

Sūrah al-Muʾmin (verse 16) goes even further than this. On the Day of Reckoning, it says, when everybody will be exposed, when secrets will be unravelled and when dissimulation will not work, Allah the Exalted will question humanity. He will ask: Whose Sovereignty prevails today? And the peoples of the world will unanimously respond: to Allah it belongs, whose dominion prevails over all false contenders.

This *āyah* received its best explanation from a *ḥadīth* reported by Imām Aḥmad ibn Ḥanbal on the authority of ʿAbdullāh ibn ʿUmar whereby the Prophet said: holding the earth and the heavens in His fist, Allah the Exalted would say: I am the King, I am the *Jabbār*, I am the *Mutakabbir*. Where are the ones who ascribed to themselves kingdoms on the earth? Where are the *jabbār*? Where are the *mutakabbir*? ʿAbdullāh ibn ʿUmar also said that the Prophet's body shook so violently, with fear, when he heard this that we thought he might fall.

Rabb

THE WORD *Rabb* is rooted in the phonals *rā-bā-bā*. Its first imprint is that of a person who brings up someone morally and physically. Later, expressions like usufruct, guardianship, reformation, and completion also sprang from it. Then, based on these meanings concepts like superiority, dominance, possession, and lordship grew. A few examples of *Rabb*'s lexicographic usage are as follows.

First, to bring up and help someone grow is an essential part of *Rabb*. For example, *Rabīb* and *Rabībah* are used for an adopted boy and girl. The adjective *Rabīb* is also used for a child who is in the custodial care of his stepfather. The nurse who looks after a child is also known as *Rabībah*. The foster mother is named as *Rābbah* for she fosters someone else's child. In the same sense, a foster father is called *Rābb*. *Murabbab* or *murabbā* is a medication preserved for safe-keeping. The verbs *Rabba*, *yurabbu*, *Rabban* are employed in the sense of growth, augmentation, and completion. For example, *Rabb al-niʿmah* means increasing one's goodness to others or being extremely generous in one's dispensation.

Second, to help converge all bits that are scattered, to consolidate and provide for also fall within *Rabb*'s ambit.

For example

فُلاَنٌ يَرُبُّ النَّاسَ

fulān yarubbun nās – means that a certain person brings other people together or people converge on his call.

The place of convergence is called *marabb* and the act of convergence is known as *tarabbub*.

Three, to look after someone, to improve a person's situation, and to provide for and superintend someone are auxiliary uses of the word *rabb*.

For example, the expression

$$\text{رَبَّ ضَيْعَتَهُ}$$

Rabba ḍayʿatahū – means that a named person looked after someone else's property.

In the Battle of Ḥunayn, Safwān is reported to have said to Abū Sufyān that:

$$\text{يَرُبَّنِي رَجُلٌ مِنْ قُرَيْشٍ أَحَبُّ إِلَيَّ مِنْ أَنْ يَرُبَّنِي رَجُلٌ مِنْ هَوَازِنَ}$$

– he would prefer to receive custodial care from a Qurayshi man than from a Hawāzin:

Says ʿAlqamah ibn ʿUbaydah:

$$\text{وَكُنْتُ امْرَءًا أَفَضْتُ إِلَيْك رَبَابَتِي}$$

$$\text{وَقَبْلَكَ رَبَّتْنِي فَضِعْتُ رُبُوبِي}$$

I have lost the rich man preceding you, who was my beneficent patron (*Murabbī*). Now my upkeep and well-being have fallen into your hands.

Says Farazdaq:

$$\text{كَأُنُوا كَسَائِلَةٍ حَمْقَاءَ إِذَا حَقَنَتْ}$$

$$\text{سَلاءَهَا فِي أَدِيمٍ غَيْرِ مَرْبُوبٍ}$$

They were like a stupid female clarifying butter, when she collected her clarifying butter in a skin not seasoned with rob.

In this couplet, *adīm ghayra marbūb* stands for a piece of leather which has not been cleansed or tanned for use.

Likewise,

$$\text{فُلَانٌ يَرُبُّ صَنْعَتَهُ عِنْدَ فُلَانٍ}$$

fulān yarubbu ṣanʿatahū ʿinda fulān – means he pursues his trade with a certain person or he receives training in a skill from that person.

Fourth, the lexicon also allows for a meaning like dominance, leadership, to command usufruct, and so forth.

For example, the expression

$$\text{قَدْ رَبَّ فُلَانٌ قَوْمَهُ}$$

qad rabba fulān qawmuhū – means that a certain person subjected his nation to his will.

Likewise, the expression

$$\text{رَبَّيْتُ القَوْمَ}$$

Rabbaytu al-qawma – means I enforced my command on my nation and overpowered it.

Says Labīd ibn Rabīʿah:

$$\text{وَأَهْلَكْنَ يَوْمًا رَبَّ كِنْدَةَ وابْنَهُ}$$
$$\text{ورَبَّ مَعَدٍّ بَيْنَ خَبْتٍ وعَرْعَرِ}$$

One day they destroyed the chief of kindah and his son and the chief of Maʿad between Khabt and ʿArʿar.

In the preceding couplet, *Rabba kinda* means the chieftain whose writ was honoured by his tribe. In the same context, we have Nābighah Dhubyānī's couplet:

$$\text{تَخُبُّ إلى النُّعْمَانِ حَتَّى تَنَالَهُ}$$
$$\text{فِدًى لَكَ مِنْ رَبٍّ تَلِيدِي وَطَارِفِي}$$

The word *Rabb* also entails ownership. For example, a *ḥadīth* says that a person asked the Prophet (*ṣallal-Lāhu ʿalayhi wa-sallam*):

$$أَرَبُّ غَنَمٍ أَمْ رَبُّ إِبِلٍ$$

are you the master of the goats or the camels?

In the same context, the master of the house is called.

رَبُّ الدَّارِ   *rabb al-dār.*

the master of the camel – رَبُّ النَّاقَة   *rabb al-nāqah.*

the master of the property – رَبُّ الضَّيْعَه   *rabb al-ḍayʿah.*

The same meaning is applicable to the master as opposed to the *ʿabd* (slave).

By repeated misuse over the years the meaning of the word *Rabb* has been reduced to one who provides, i.e. the provider.

However, in a cumulative sense, when all its various meanings are considered, the word rather bridges a broad-based concept that covers the following range of meanings:

• He who nourishes and dispenses needs, brings up morally and physically.

• He who takes care, supervises, and is responsible for improving the situation.

• He who has the axial position upon whom divergence converges.

• He who is the noblest and the source of power and authority; whose writ prevails and who is the wielder of dispensation.

• He who is the owner and the master.

Qur'ānic use of the word *rabb*

Qur'ānic use of the word *Rabb* involves all of the meanings identified above. Sometimes it conjoins one or two meanings; and on occasions, it embraces several. In yet another context, *Rabb* is also used in the sense of Owner and Master. We will, however, explain *Rabb*'s use in the Qur'ān by means of the following *āyahs*:

In the first meaning where *Rabb* equates with a nourisher and dispenser of needs, the Qur'ān says:

وَرَٰوَدَتْهُ ٱلَّتِي هُوَ فِي بَيْتِهَا عَن نَّفْسِهِۦ وَغَلَّقَتِ ٱلْأَبْوَٰبَ وَقَالَتْ هَيْتَ لَكَ ۚ
قَالَ مَعَاذَ ٱللَّهِ ۖ إِنَّهُۥ رَبِّيٓ أَحْسَنَ مَثْوَايَ ۖ إِنَّهُۥ لَا يُفْلِحُ ٱلظَّٰلِمُونَ ﴿٢٣﴾

But she in whose house he was, sought to seduce him from his (true) self: she fastened the doors, and said: "Now come, you (dear one)!" He said: "Allah forbid! Truly (your husband) is my lord! He made my sojourn agreeable! Truly to no good come those who do wrong!"

Yūsuf 12:23

The second meaning of *Rabb* – namely, as a carer, supervisor and someone who is responsible – embraces the first as well:

فَإِنَّهُمْ عَدُوٌّ لِّيٓ إِلَّا رَبَّ ٱلْعَٰلَمِينَ ﴿٧٧﴾ ٱلَّذِى خَلَقَنِي فَهُوَ يَهْدِينِ ﴿٧٨﴾ وَٱلَّذِى
هُوَ يُطْعِمُنِي وَيَسْقِينِ ﴿٧٩﴾ وَإِذَا مَرِضْتُ فَهُوَ يَشْفِينِ ﴿٨٠﴾

"For they are enemies to me; not so the Lord and Cherisher of the Worlds; Who created me, and it is He Who guides me; Who gives me food and drink. And when I am ill, it is He Who cures me."

al-Shuʿarā' 26:77–80

وَمَا بِكُم مِّن نِّعْمَةٍ فَمِنَ ٱللَّهِ ثُمَّ إِذَا مَسَّكُمُ ٱلضُّرُّ فَإِلَيْهِ تَجْـَٔرُونَ ٥٣ ثُمَّ إِذَا كَشَفَ ٱلضُّرَّ عَنكُمْ إِذَا فَرِيقٌ مِّنكُم بِرَبِّهِمْ يُشْرِكُونَ ٥٤

And you have no good thing but is from Allah: and moreover,
when you are touched by distress, unto Him you cry with
groans; yet, when He removes the distress from you, behold!
some of you turn to other gods to join with their Lord.

al-Naḥl 16:53-54

قُلْ أَغَيْرَ ٱللَّهِ أَبْغِي رَبًّا وَهُوَ رَبُّ كُلِّ شَيْءٍ وَلَا تَكْسِبُ كُلُّ نَفْسٍ إِلَّا عَلَيْهَا وَلَا تَزِرُ وَازِرَةٌ وِزْرَ أُخْرَىٰ ثُمَّ إِلَىٰ رَبِّكُم مَّرْجِعُكُمْ فَيُنَبِّئُكُم بِمَا كُنتُمْ فِيهِ تَخْتَلِفُونَ ١٦٤

Say: "Shall I seek for (my) Cherisher other than Allah,
when He is the Cherisher of all things (that exist)? Every
soul draws the meed of its acts on none but itself: no bearer
of burdens can bear the burden of another. Your goal in the
end is towards Allah: He will tell you the truth of the things
wherein you disputed."

al-An'ām 6:164

رَّبُّ ٱلْمَشْرِقِ وَٱلْمَغْرِبِ لَا إِلَٰهَ إِلَّا هُوَ فَٱتَّخِذْهُ وَكِيلًا ٩

(He is) Lord of the East and the West: there is no god but
He: take Him therefore for (your) Disposer of Affairs.

al-Muzzammil 73:9

The third meaning, of he who holds the axial position, stands
by itself:

وَلَا يَنفَعُكُمْ نُصْحِى إِنْ أَرَدتُّ أَنْ أَنصَحَ لَكُمْ إِن كَانَ اللَّهُ يُرِيدُ أَن يُغْوِيَكُمْ هُوَ رَبُّكُمْ وَإِلَيْهِ تُرْجَعُونَ ۝

"Of no profit will be my counsel to you, much as I desire to give you (good) counsel, if it be that Allah wills to leave you astray: He is your Lord! and to Him will you return!"

Hūd 11:34

إِن تَكْفُرُوا۟ فَإِنَّ اللَّهَ غَنِىٌّ عَنكُمْ وَلَا يَرْضَىٰ لِعِبَادِهِ الْكُفْرَ وَإِن تَشْكُرُوا۟ يَرْضَهُ لَكُمْ وَلَا تَزِرُ وَازِرَةٌ وِزْرَ أُخْرَىٰ ثُمَّ إِلَىٰ رَبِّكُم مَّرْجِعُكُمْ فَيُنَبِّئُكُم بِمَا كُنتُمْ تَعْمَلُونَ إِنَّهُۥ عَلِيمٌۢ بِذَاتِ الصُّدُورِ ۝

If you reject (Allah), truly Allah has no need of you; but He likes not ingratitude from His servants: if you are grateful, He is pleased with you. No bearer of burdens can bear the burden of another. In the end, to your Lord is your return, when He will tell you the truth of all that you did (in this life). For He knows well all that is in (men's) hearts.

al-Zumar 39:7

قُل يَجْمَعُ بَيْنَنَا رَبُّنَا ثُمَّ يَفْتَحُ بَيْنَنَا بِالْحَقِّ وَهُوَ الْفَتَّاحُ الْعَلِيمُ ۝

Say: "Our Lord shall assemble us together, then He shall judge between us with truth; and He is the great judge, the All-Knowing."

Saba' 34:26

وَمَا مِن دَآبَّةٍ فِى ٱلْأَرْضِ وَلَا طَـٰٓئِرٍ يَطِيرُ بِجَنَاحَيْهِ إِلَّآ أُمَمٌ أَمْثَالُكُم ۚ
مَّا فَرَّطْنَا فِى ٱلْكِتَـٰبِ مِن شَىْءٍ ۚ ثُمَّ إِلَىٰ رَبِّهِمْ يُحْشَرُونَ ۝

There is not an animal (that lives) on the earth, nor a being
that flies on its wings, but (forms part of) communities like
you. Nothing have We omitted from the Book, and they (all)
shall be gathered to their Lord in the end.

al-An'ām 6:38

وَنُفِخَ فِى ٱلصُّورِ فَإِذَا هُم مِّنَ ٱلْأَجْدَاثِ إِلَىٰ رَبِّهِمْ يَنسِلُونَ ۝

The trumpet shall be sounded, when behold! from the
sepulchres (men) will rush forth to their Lord!

Yā Sīn 36:51

The fourth meaning of *Rabb* as the source of power conjoins the
third as well:

ٱتَّخَذُوٓاْ أَحْبَارَهُمْ وَرُهْبَـٰنَهُمْ أَرْبَابًا مِّن دُونِ ٱللَّهِ وَٱلْمَسِيحَ ٱبْنَ مَرْيَمَ
وَمَآ أُمِرُوٓاْ إِلَّا لِيَعْبُدُوٓاْ إِلَـٰهًا وَٰحِدًا ۖ لَّآ إِلَـٰهَ إِلَّا هُوَ ۚ سُبْحَـٰنَهُۥ
عَمَّا يُشْرِكُونَ ۝

They have taken their priests and their monks for their lords
besides Allah, and also the Messiah, son of Mary, whereas
they were commanded to worship none but the One True
God. There is no god but He. Exalted be He above those
whom they associate with Him in His Divinity.

al-Tawbah 9:31

قُلْ يَـٰٓأَهْلَ ٱلْكِتَـٰبِ تَعَالَوْاْ إِلَىٰ كَلِمَةٍ سَوَآءٍ بَيْنَنَا وَبَيْنَكُمْ أَلَّا نَعْبُدَ إِلَّا ٱللَّهَ وَلَا نُشْرِكَ بِهِۦ شَيْـًٔا وَلَا يَتَّخِذَ بَعْضُنَا بَعْضًا أَرْبَابًا مِّن دُونِ ٱللَّهِ فَإِن تَوَلَّوْاْ فَقُولُواْ ٱشْهَدُواْ بِأَنَّا مُسْلِمُونَ ۝

Say: "People of the Book! Come to a word common between
us and you: that we shall serve none but Allah and shall
associate none with Him in His Divinity and that some of
us will not take others as lords other than Allah." And if
they turn away (from accepting this call), tell them: "Bear
witness that we are the ones who have submitted ourselves
exclusively to Allah."

Āl ʿImrān 3:64

In both these *āyahs arbāb* means people whom nations and groups
elevate to the absolute rank of leaders and religious icons whose
commands, rules and regulations, and prohibitory and permissible
measures are accepted without grudge.

وَقَالَ لِلَّذِى ظَنَّ أَنَّهُۥ نَاجٍ مِّنْهُمَا ٱذْكُرْنِى عِندَ رَبِّكَ فَأَنسَىٰهُ ٱلشَّيْطَـٰنُ ذِكْرَ رَبِّهِۦ فَلَبِثَ فِى ٱلسِّجْنِ بِضْعَ سِنِينَ ۝

And Joseph said to the one of the two prisoners who he knew
would be set free: "Mention me in your lord's presence."
But Satan caused him to forget mentioning this to his lord
(the ruler of Egypt) and so Joseph languished in prison for
several years.

Yūsuf 12:42

وَقَالَ ٱلْمَلِكُ ٱئْتُونِى بِهِۦ فَلَمَّا جَآءَهُ ٱلرَّسُولُ قَالَ ٱرْجِعْ إِلَىٰ رَبِّكَ فَسْـَٔلْهُ مَا بَالُ ٱلنِّسْوَةِ ٱلَّـٰتِى قَطَّعْنَ أَيْدِيَهُنَّ إِنَّ رَبِّى بِكَيْدِهِنَّ عَلِيمٌ ۝

The king said: "Bring this man to me." But when the royal
messenger came to Joseph he said: "Go back to your master
and ask him about the case of the women who had cut their
hands. Surely my Lord has full knowledge of their guile."

Yūsuf 12: 50

In these *āyahs*, the Prophet Yūsuf (the biblical Joseph) repeatedly
declares that the Egyptians perceived Pharaoh as their *Rabb*. This
description was apt because the Egyptians did accept Pharaoh's
centrality, his sovereignty and his status as a lawgiver who regulated
their lives. At the same time, however, the Prophet Yūsuf acknowledged
Allah as his *Rabb*, for he considered Allah and not Pharaoh as his
Sovereign and Lawgiver.

The following *āyahs* incorporate the concept of *Rabb* in the fifth
sense as owner and master: *al-Quraysh* 106:3-4; *al-Anbiyā'* 21:2; *al-
Mu'minūn* 23:5; *al-Ṣāffāt* 37:1 and *al-Najm* 53:3.

The fifth meaning of *Rabb* as owner and master also conjoins
the third:

$$\text{فَلْيَعْبُدُواْ رَبَّ هَـٰذَا ٱلْبَيْتِ ۝ ٱلَّذِىٓ أَطْعَمَهُم مِّن جُوعٍ وَءَامَنَهُم مِّنْ خَوْفِۭ ۝}$$

Let them adore the Lord of this House, Who provides them
with food against hunger, and with security against fear (of
danger).

al-Quraysh 106:3-4

$$\text{سُبْحَـٰنَ رَبِّكَ رَبِّ ٱلْعِزَّةِ عَمَّا يَصِفُونَ ۝}$$

Glory to your Lord, the Lord of Honour and Power! (He is
free) from what they ascribe (to Him)!

al-Ṣāffāt 37:180

$$\text{لَوْ كَانَ فِيهِمَا ءَالِهَةٌ إِلَّا ٱللَّهُ لَفَسَدَتَا فَسُبْحَـٰنَ ٱللَّهِ رَبِّ ٱلْعَرْشِ عَمَّا يَصِفُونَ ۝}$$

If there were, in the heavens and the earth, other gods besides Allah, there would have been confusion in both! But glory to Allah, the Lord of the Throne: (High is He) above what they attribute to Him!

al-Anbiyā' 21:22

$$\text{قُلْ مَن رَّبُّ ٱلسَّمَـٰوَٰتِ ٱلسَّبْعِ وَرَبُّ ٱلْعَرْشِ ٱلْعَظِيمِ ۝}$$

Say: "Who is the Lord of the seven heavens, and the Lord of the Throne (of Glory) Supreme?"

al-Mu'minūn 23:86

$$\text{رَبُّ ٱلسَّمَـٰوَٰتِ وَٱلْأَرْضِ وَمَا بَيْنَهُمَا وَرَبُّ ٱلْمَشَـٰرِقِ ۝}$$

Lord of the heavens and of the earth, and all between them, and Lord of every point at the rising of the sun!

al-Ṣāffāt 37:5

$$\text{وَأَنَّهُ هُوَ رَبُّ ٱلشِّعْرَىٰ ۝}$$

That He is the Lord of Sirius (the Mighty Star).

al-Najm 53:49

Rubūbīyah (divinity) as understood by nations that strayed in the past

Having established the meanings of the word *Rabb*, we now need to focus on the distorted views of *rubūbīyah* (divinity) that caused the Qur'ānic descent in the first place. Furthermore, we also need to explore what exactly it was that the Qur'ān invited people towards.

In order to do this we first need to deal with the mindset of past nations that had strayed and about which the Qur'ān speaks, so that the concept of *rubūbīyah* becomes clear.

Nūḥ's people

The Qur'ān takes up the case of Nūḥ's (the biblical Noah) people first. These people, as the Qur'ān tells us, did not deny Allah's existence:

فَقَالَ ٱلۡمَلَؤُاْ ٱلَّذِينَ كَفَرُواْ مِن قَوۡمِهِۦ مَا هَٰذَآ إِلَّا بَشَرٞ مِّثۡلُكُمۡ يُرِيدُ
أَن يَتَفَضَّلَ عَلَيۡكُمۡ وَلَوۡ شَآءَ ٱللَّهُ لَأَنزَلَ مَلَٰٓئِكَةٗ مَّا سَمِعۡنَا بِهَٰذَا
فِىٓ ءَابَآئِنَا ٱلۡأَوَّلِينَ ۝

The chiefs of the Unbelievers among his people said: "He is no more than a man like yourselves: his wish is to assert his superiority over you: if Allah had wished (to send messengers), He could have sent down angels: never did we hear such a thing (as he says), among our ancestors of old."

al-Mu'minūn 23:24

It is obvious from this that they did not deny Allah as their Creator. Nor did they refuse to acknowledge Him as their *Rabb* in the first and the second senses. Thus, Noah says to them:

وَلَا يَنفَعُكُمۡ نُصۡحِىٓ إِنۡ أَرَدتُّ أَنۡ أَنصَحَ لَكُمۡ إِن كَانَ ٱللَّهُ يُرِيدُ أَن
يُغۡوِيَكُمۡ هُوَ رَبُّكُمۡ وَإِلَيۡهِ تُرۡجَعُونَ ۝

"He is your Lord! And to Him will you return!"

Hūd 11:34

فَقُلۡتُ ٱسۡتَغۡفِرُواْ رَبَّكُمۡ إِنَّهُۥ كَانَ غَفَّارٗا ۝

Saying: 'Ask forgiveness from your Lord; for He is Oft-Forgiving.'

Nūḥ 71:10

أَلَمۡ تَرَوۡاْ كَيۡفَ خَلَقَ ٱللَّهُ سَبۡعَ سَمَٰوَٰتٖ طِبَاقٗا ۝ وَجَعَلَ ٱلۡقَمَرَ فِيهِنَّ نُورٗا
وَجَعَلَ ٱلشَّمۡسَ سِرَاجٗا ۝

See you not how Allah has created the seven heavens one
above another, and made the moon a light in their midst,
and made the sun as a (Glorious) Lamp?

Nūḥ 71:15-16

None of them denies Allah as their *Rabb* nor do they discount
Allah's creativity and their origination at His hands. Nor do they
counter Noah by attributing the management of the universe to
someone other than Allah.

Likewise, they did not deny Allah as their *Ilāh*. Hence why Noah
phrased his call in these words: *mā lakum min ilāhin ghayruhū* – you
do not have an *ilāh* other than Him. For if they had denied Allah as
their *Ilāh*, the call would have been phrased as follows: *ittakhadhū
Allāha ilāhan* – accept Allah as your *Ilāh*.

The question, then, is: what exactly was the conflict between
Noah and his people? From the Qur'ān it appears that this involved
two aspects. First, Noah demanded that people should discard
other *ilāh*s and surrender themselves to the One whom they already
acknowledged as Life Giver to everything in the universe, and Who
alone is the Dispenser of needs.

لَقَدْ أَرْسَلْنَا نُوحًا إِلَىٰ قَوْمِهِ فَقَالَ يَـٰقَوْمِ ٱعْبُدُواْ ٱللَّهَ مَا لَكُم مِّنْ إِلَـٰهٍ
غَيْرُهُۥٓ إِنِّىٓ أَخَافُ عَلَيْكُمْ عَذَابَ يَوْمٍ عَظِيمٍ ۞ قَالَ ٱلْمَلَأُ مِن قَوْمِهِۦٓ إِنَّا
لَنَرَىٰكَ فِى ضَلَـٰلٍ مُّبِينٍ ۞ قَالَ يَـٰقَوْمِ لَيْسَ بِى ضَلَـٰلَةٌ وَلَـٰكِنِّى رَسُولٌ
مِّن رَّبِّ ٱلْعَـٰلَمِينَ ۞ أُبَلِّغُكُمْ رِسَـٰلَـٰتِ رَبِّى وَأَنصَحُ لَكُمْ وَأَعْلَمُ مِنَ
ٱللَّهِ مَا لَا تَعْلَمُونَ ۞

We sent Noah to his people. He said: "O my people! Worship
Allah! You have no other god but Him. I fear for you the
punishment of a dreadful day!" The leaders of his people
said: "Ah! We see you evidently wandering (in mind)." He
said: "O my people! No wandering is there in my (mind): on
the contrary I am a messenger from the Lord and Cherisher

of the Worlds! I but fulfil towards you the duties of my Lord's mission: sincere is my advice to you, and I know from Allah something that you know not."

al-A'rāf 7:59-62

In turn, although his people insisted that everything belonged to Allah – the Master and the Sovereign – there were others as well who shared His kingdom. As such, they were also the focus of their longings. This, thus demonstrates that besides Allah they also embraced other *ilāh*s as well.

وَقَالُواْ لَا تَذَرُنَّ ءَالِهَتَكُمْ وَلَا تَذَرُنَّ وَدًّا وَلَا سُوَاعًا وَلَا يَغُوثَ وَيَعُوقَ وَنَسْرًا ۝

"And they have said (to each other), 'Abandon not your gods: abandon neither Wadd nor Suwā', neither Yaghūth nor Ya'ūq, nor Nasr'"

Nūḥ 71:23

Second, they took Allah as their *Rabb* in the sense that He was their Creator, the Master of the universe and its Executor. But at the same time, they excluded God from the realm of ethics, society, civilization, politics and other aspects of worldly life. They did not believe that God was the fount of everything – their Guide, Legislator, and Arbiter of right and wrong; or that to Him alone was obedience and compliance due. In all these aspects of authority, they had elevated their elders and religious hierarchy to divinity. In this respect, then, the Prophet Noah warned them not to splinter the concept of *rubūbīyah* into several entities and instead accept Allah as their *Rabb* by embracing His laws and injunctions delivered by him on His behalf.

إِنِّى لَكُمْ رَسُولٌ أَمِينٌ ۝ فَٱتَّقُواْ ٱللَّهَ وَأَطِيعُونِ ۝

"I am to you a messenger worthy of all trust: so fear Allah, and obey me."

al-Shu'arā' 26:107-108

The ‘Ād

The Qur’ān also mentions the ‘Ād. Like Noah’s nation, they too believed in Allah’s existence and His being *Ilāh*. They also accepted Allah as their *Rabb* but not surprisingly also held the same contentious views that Noah’s people had earlier verbalized. The Qur’ān projects their state of mind thus:

۞ وَإِلَىٰ عَادٍ أَخَاهُمْ هُودًا قَالَ يَٰقَوْمِ ٱعْبُدُوا۟ ٱللَّهَ مَا لَكُم مِّنْ إِلَٰهٍ غَيْرُهُ أَفَلَا تَتَّقُونَ ۞ قَالَ ٱلْمَلَأُ ٱلَّذِينَ كَفَرُوا۟ مِن قَوْمِهِ إِنَّا لَنَرَىٰكَ فِى سَفَاهَةٍ وَإِنَّا لَنَظُنُّكَ مِنَ ٱلْكَٰذِبِينَ ۞ قَالَ يَٰقَوْمِ لَيْسَ بِى سَفَاهَةٌ وَلَٰكِنِّى رَسُولٌ مِّن رَّبِّ ٱلْعَٰلَمِينَ ۞ أُبَلِّغُكُمْ رِسَٰلَٰتِ رَبِّى وَأَنَا۠ لَكُمْ نَاصِحٌ أَمِينٌ ۞ أَوَعَجِبْتُمْ أَن جَآءَكُمْ ذِكْرٌ مِّن رَّبِّكُمْ عَلَىٰ رَجُلٍ مِّنكُمْ لِيُنذِرَكُمْ وَٱذْكُرُوٓا۟ إِذْ جَعَلَكُمْ خُلَفَآءَ مِنۢ بَعْدِ قَوْمِ نُوحٍ وَزَادَكُمْ فِى ٱلْخَلْقِ بَصْۜطَةً فَٱذْكُرُوٓا۟ ءَالَآءَ ٱللَّهِ لَعَلَّكُمْ تُفْلِحُونَ ۞ قَالُوٓا۟ أَجِئْتَنَا لِنَعْبُدَ ٱللَّهَ وَحْدَهُ وَنَذَرَ مَا كَانَ يَعْبُدُ ءَابَآؤُنَا فَأْتِنَا بِمَا تَعِدُنَآ إِن كُنتَ مِنَ ٱلصَّٰدِقِينَ ۞

To the ‘Ād people, (We sent) Hūd, one of their (own) brethren: he said: "O my people! Worship Allah! You have no other god but Him. Will you not fear (Allah)?" The leaders of the unbelievers among his people said: "Ah! We see you are an imbecile!" and "We think you are a liar!" He said: "O my people! I am no imbecile, but (I am) a messenger from the Lord and Cherisher of the Worlds! I but fulfil towards you the duties of my Lord’s mission: I am to you a sincere and trustworthy adviser. Do you wonder that there has come to you a message from your Lord through a man of your own people, to warn you? Call in remembrance that He made you inheritors after the people of Noah, and gave you a stature tall among the nations. Call in remembrance the benefits (you have received) from Allah: that so you may prosper." They said: "Come you to us, that we may worship Allah alone, and give up the cult of our fathers: bring us what you threaten us with, if it so be that you tell the truth!"

al-A'rāf 7:65-70

إِذْ جَاءَتْهُمُ ٱلرُّسُلُ مِنْ بَيْنِ أَيْدِيهِمْ وَمِنْ خَلْفِهِمْ أَلَّا تَعْبُدُوٓاْ إِلَّا ٱللَّهَ قَالُواْ لَوْ شَآءَ رَبُّنَا لَأَنزَلَ مَلَـٰٓئِكَةً فَإِنَّا بِمَآ أُرْسِلْتُم بِهِۦ كَـٰفِرُونَ ۝

Behold, the messengers came to them, from before them and behind them, (preaching): "Serve none but Allah." They said, "If our Lord had so pleased, He would certainly have sent down angels (to preach): now we reject your mission (altogether)."

Fuṣṣilat 41:14

وَتِلْكَ عَادٌ جَحَدُواْ بِـَٔايَـٰتِ رَبِّهِمْ وَعَصَوْاْ رُسُلَهُۥ وَٱتَّبَعُوٓاْ أَمْرَ كُلِّ جَبَّارٍ عَنِيدٍ ۝

Such were the 'Ād. They opposed the signs of their Lord and denied His Messengers and followed the bidding of any tyrant.

Hūd 11:59

The Thamūd

Similar to the 'Ād, the Thamūd had also cultivated rebellious attitudes. In essence, their depravity was like others before them: they did not deny Allah's existence or His providence; nor did they deny Him worship. So what exactly was it that they denied? First, they refused to accept Allah as the *Ilāh* Who alone deserved worship.

Second, they did not believe that *rubūbīyah* in its extended sense was exclusive to Allah. Hence why, besides Allah, they turned to others as problem solvers and dispensers of relief and comfort. They also bypassed Allah and insisted on following their elders and religious leaders. Essentially, then, their attitudes qualified them for Divine punishment. The Qur'ān speaks of this as follows:

فَإِنْ أَعْرَضُوا فَقُلْ أَنذَرْتُكُمْ صَٰعِقَةً مِّثْلَ صَٰعِقَةِ عَادٍ وَثَمُودَ ۝ إِذْ جَآءَتْهُمُ الرُّسُلُ مِنۢ بَيْنِ أَيْدِيهِمْ وَمِنْ خَلْفِهِمْ أَلَّا تَعْبُدُوٓا۟ إِلَّا ٱللَّهَ قَالُوا۟ لَوْ شَآءَ رَبُّنَا لَأَنزَلَ مَلَٰٓئِكَةً فَإِنَّا بِمَآ أُرْسِلْتُم بِهِۦ كَٰفِرُونَ ۝

But if they turn away, say you: "I have warned you of a stunning punishment (as of thunder and lightning) like that which (overtook) the 'Ād and the Thamūd!" Behold, the messengers came to them, from before them and behind them, (preaching): "Serve none but Allah." They said, "If our Lord had so pleased, He would certainly have sent down angels (to preach): now we reject your mission (altogether)."

Fuṣṣilat 41:13-14

۞ وَإِلَىٰ ثَمُودَ أَخَاهُمْ صَٰلِحًا قَالَ يَٰقَوْمِ ٱعْبُدُوا۟ ٱللَّهَ مَا لَكُم مِّنْ إِلَٰهٍ غَيْرُهُۥ هُوَ أَنشَأَكُم مِّنَ ٱلْأَرْضِ وَٱسْتَعْمَرَكُمْ فِيهَا فَٱسْتَغْفِرُوهُ ثُمَّ تُوبُوٓا۟ إِلَيْهِ إِنَّ رَبِّى قَرِيبٌ مُّجِيبٌ ۝ قَالُوا۟ يَٰصَٰلِحُ قَدْ كُنتَ فِينَا مَرْجُوًّا قَبْلَ هَٰذَآ أَتَنْهَىٰنَآ أَن نَّعْبُدَ مَا يَعْبُدُ ءَابَآؤُنَا وَإِنَّنَا لَفِى شَكٍّ مِّمَّا تَدْعُونَآ إِلَيْهِ مُرِيبٍ ۝

To the Thamūd people (We sent) Ṣāliḥ, one of their own brethren. He said "O my People! Worship Allah: you have no other god but Him. It is He Who has produced you from the earth and settled you therein: then ask forgiveness of Him, and turn to Him (in repentance): for my Lord is (always) near, ready to answer." They said: "O Ṣāliḥ! You have been of us! – a centre of our hopes hitherto! Do you (now) forbid us the worship of what our fathers worshipped? But we are really in suspicious (disquieting) doubt as to that to which you invite us."

Hūd 11:61-62

إِذْ قَالَ لَهُمْ أَخُوهُمْ صَـٰلِحٌ أَلَا تَتَّقُونَ ۞ إِنِّى لَكُمْ رَسُولٌ أَمِينٌ ۞ فَٱتَّقُواْ ٱللَّهَ وَأَطِيعُونِ ۞ وَمَآ أَسْـَٔلُكُمْ عَلَيْهِ مِنْ أَجْرٍ إِنْ أَجْرِىَ إِلَّا عَلَىٰ رَبِّ ٱلْعَـٰلَمِينَ ۞ أَتُتْرَكُونَ فِى مَا هَـٰهُنَآ ءَامِنِينَ ۞ فِى جَنَّـٰتٍ وَعُيُونٍ ۞ وَزُرُوعٍ وَنَخْلٍ طَلْعُهَا هَضِيمٌ ۞ وَتَنْحِتُونَ مِنَ ٱلْجِبَالِ بُيُوتًا فَـٰرِهِينَ ۞ فَٱتَّقُواْ ٱللَّهَ وَأَطِيعُونِ ۞ وَلَا تُطِيعُوٓاْ أَمْرَ ٱلْمُسْرِفِينَ ۞ ٱلَّذِينَ يُفْسِدُونَ فِى ٱلْأَرْضِ وَلَا يُصْلِحُونَ ۞

Behold, their brother Ṣāliḥ said to them: "Will you not fear (Allah)? I am to you a messenger worthy of all trust. So fear Allah, and obey me. No reward do I ask of you for it: my reward is only from the Lord of the Worlds. Will you be left secure, in (the enjoyment of) all that you have here? – gardens and springs, and cornfields and date palms with spathes near breaking (with the weight of fruit)? And you carve houses out of (rocky) mountains with great skill. But fear Allah and obey me; and follow not the bidding of those who are extravagant – who make mischief in the land, and mend not (their ways)."

al-Shuʿarā' 26:142-152

The people of Ibrāhīm and Nimrūd

The case of Ibrāhīm's people (the biblical Abraham) is of particular significance owing to a commonplace misperception that their king, Nimrod, denied God and instead proclaimed himself a god. In fact, he did believe in Allah's existence and His corresponding attributes of Creator and Administrator of the universe. His problem was that he projected himself as *ilāh* in the third, fourth and the fifth senses of the word *Rabb*. Besides, it is also wrong to think that the Abrahamic people were ignorant of Allah and denied Him divinity. What depravity they displayed was marked by their belief in the divinity of celestial bodies followed by their belief in their king as *Rabb*. The Qur'ānic account of their beliefs is uncommonly vivid. Let us first take the episode of Ibrāhīm's adolescence, which gives us an insight into his search for the truth:

فَلَمَّا جَنَّ عَلَيْهِ ٱلَّيْلُ رَءَا كَوْكَبًا قَالَ هَـٰذَا رَبِّى فَلَمَّآ أَفَلَ قَالَ لَآ أُحِبُّ ٱلْأَفِلِينَ ۝ فَلَمَّا رَءَا ٱلْقَمَرَ بَازِغًا قَالَ هَـٰذَا رَبِّى فَلَمَّآ أَفَلَ قَالَ لَئِن لَّمْ يَهْدِنِى رَبِّى لَأَكُونَنَّ مِنَ ٱلْقَوْمِ ٱلضَّآلِّينَ ۝ فَلَمَّا رَءَا ٱلشَّمْسَ بَازِغَةً قَالَ هَـٰذَا رَبِّى هَـٰذَآ أَكْبَرُ فَلَمَّآ أَفَلَتْ قَالَ يَـٰقَوْمِ إِنِّى بَرِىٓءٌ مِّمَّا تُشْرِكُونَ ۝ إِنِّى وَجَّهْتُ وَجْهِىَ لِلَّذِى فَطَرَ ٱلسَّمَـٰوَٰتِ وَٱلْأَرْضَ حَنِيفًا وَمَآ أَنَا۠ مِنَ ٱلْمُشْرِكِينَ ۝

When the night covered him over, he saw a star: he said: "This is my Lord." But when it set, he said: "I love not those that set." When he saw the moon rising in splendour, he said: "This is my Lord." But when the moon set, he said: "Unless my Lord guide me, I shall surely be among those who go astray." When he saw the sun rising in splendour, he said: "This is my Lord; this is the greatest (of all)." But when the sun set, he said: "O my people! I am indeed free from your (guilt) of giving partners to Allah. For me, I have set my face, firmly and truly, towards Him Who created the heavens and the earth, and never shall I give partners to Allah."

al-Anʿām 6:76-79

The society that parented Ibrāhīm was familiar with the concept of *rubūbīyah* as distinct from their belief in the divinity of celestial bodies. This should not be surprising as their heritage was Islamic: their elders had in the past embraced Islam in response to Noah's call. Further, their nearest neighbours, the ʿĀd and Thamūd, had experienced true Islam through the frequent mediation of the prophets among them.

Thus, the Prophet Ibrāhīm had received the primary concept of Allah as the Creator and the Master of the heavens and the earth and of His being the *Rabb*. What, however, did bother him was the prevalent notion of ascribing divinity to celestial bodies besides Allah and worshipping them. Archaeological finds support this Qur'ānic account.[1]

Thus, his search before his elevation to the prophetic office remained specific to this aspect. The rise and setting of the moon and the sun furnished him with the argument that none can qualify as *Rabb* other than the One Who owns the heavens and the earth. His observation on the moon's disappearance in the glow of the day is poignant: I am scared that if my *Rabb* (Allah) does not guide me, I will go astray by the appearance of a physical phenomena which has already misled millions. I am scared that I will not arrive at the Truth.

Likewise, after his elevation to the prophetic office, Ibrāhīm started his call to worship Allah with words that exposed this matter further:

وَكَيْفَ أَخَافُ مَا أَشْرَكْتُمْ وَلَا تَخَافُونَ أَنَّكُمْ أَشْرَكْتُم بِٱللَّهِ مَا لَمْ يُنَزِّلْ بِهِۦ عَلَيْكُمْ سُلْطَٰنًا ۚ فَأَىُّ ٱلْفَرِيقَيْنِ أَحَقُّ بِٱلْأَمْنِ ۖ إِن كُنتُمْ تَعْلَمُونَ ۝

"How should I fear (the beings) you associate with Allah, when you fear not to give partners to Allah without any warrant having been given to you? Which of (us) two parties has more right to security? (Tell me) if you know."

al-Anʿām 6:81

وَأَعْتَزِلُكُمْ وَمَا تَدْعُونَ مِن دُونِ ٱللَّهِ وَأَدْعُوا۟ رَبِّى عَسَىٰٓ أَلَّآ أَكُونَ بِدُعَآءِ رَبِّى شَقِيًّا ۝

---

1. The finds pertaining to the Prophet Ibrāhīm's era in Ur reveal that his people worshipped a moon-god, which they called "Nannār". In the neighbouring territory of Larasa, they worshipped a sun-god named Shamāsh.

"And I will turn away from you (all) and from those whom
you invoke besides Allah: I will call on my Lord: perhaps, by
my prayer to my Lord, I shall be not unblest!"

Maryam: 19:48

قَالَ بَل رَّبُّكُمْ رَبُّ ٱلسَّمَٰوَٰتِ وَٱلْأَرْضِ ٱلَّذِى فَطَرَهُنَّ وَأَنَا۠ عَلَىٰ ذَٰلِكُم
مِّنَ ٱلشَّٰهِدِينَ ۝ وَتَٱللَّهِ لَأَكِيدَنَّ أَصْنَٰمَكُم بَعْدَ أَن تُوَلُّواْ مُدْبِرِينَ ۝
فَجَعَلَهُمْ جُذَٰذًا إِلَّا كَبِيرًا لَّهُمْ لَعَلَّهُمْ إِلَيْهِ يَرْجِعُونَ ۝ قَالُواْ مَن فَعَلَ هَٰذَا
بِـَٔالِهَتِنَآ إِنَّهُۥ لَمِنَ ٱلظَّٰلِمِينَ ۝ قَالُواْ سَمِعْنَا فَتًى يَذْكُرُهُمْ يُقَالُ لَهُۥٓ
إِبْرَٰهِيمُ ۝ قَالُواْ فَأْتُواْ بِهِۦ عَلَىٰٓ أَعْيُنِ ٱلنَّاسِ لَعَلَّهُمْ يَشْهَدُونَ ۝ قَالُوٓاْ ءَأَنتَ
فَعَلْتَ هَٰذَا بِـَٔالِهَتِنَا يَٰٓإِبْرَٰهِيمُ ۝ قَالَ بَلْ فَعَلَهُۥ كَبِيرُهُمْ هَٰذَا
فَسْـَٔلُوهُمْ إِن كَانُواْ يَنطِقُونَ ۝ فَرَجَعُوٓاْ إِلَىٰٓ أَنفُسِهِمْ فَقَالُوٓاْ إِنَّكُمْ أَنتُمُ
ٱلظَّٰلِمُونَ ۝ ثُمَّ نُكِسُواْ عَلَىٰ رُءُوسِهِمْ لَقَدْ عَلِمْتَ مَا هَٰٓؤُلَآءِ يَنطِقُونَ ۝
قَالَ أَفَتَعْبُدُونَ مِن دُونِ ٱللَّهِ مَا لَا يَنفَعُكُمْ شَيْـًٔا وَلَا يَضُرُّكُمْ ۝

He said, "Nay, your Lord is the Lord of the heavens and
the earth. He Who created them (from nothing): and I am a
witness to this (truth). And by Allah, I have a plan for your
idols – after you go away and turn your backs" ... So he
broke them to pieces, (all) but the biggest of them, that they
might turn (and address themselves) to it. They said, "Who
has done this to our gods? He must indeed be some man of
impiety!" They said, "We heard a youth talk of them: he is
called Abraham." They said, "Then bring him before the
eyes of the people, that they may bear witness." They said,
"Are you the one that did this with our gods, O Abraham?"
He said: "Nay, this was done by their biggest one! So ask
them, if they can speak intelligently!" So they turned to
themselves and said, "Surely you are the ones in the wrong!"
Then were they confounded with shame: (they said) "You

know full well that these (idols) do not speak!" (Abraham)
said, "Do you then worship, besides Allah, things that can
neither be of any good to you nor do you harm?"

al-Anbiyā' 21:56-66

إِذْ قَالَ لِأَبِيهِ وَقَوْمِهِ مَاذَا تَعْبُدُونَ ۝ أَئِفْكًا ءَالِهَةً دُونَ ٱللَّهِ تُرِيدُونَ ۝
فَمَا ظَنُّكُم بِرَبِّ ٱلْعَٰلَمِينَ ۝

Behold, he said to his father and to his people, "What is that
which you worship? Is it a Falsehood – gods other than Allah
that you desire? Then what is your idea about the Lord of
the Worlds?"

al-Ṣāffāt 37:85-87

قَدْ كَانَتْ لَكُمْ أُسْوَةٌ حَسَنَةٌ فِىٓ إِبْرَٰهِيمَ وَٱلَّذِينَ مَعَهُۥ إِذْ قَالُوا۟ لِقَوْمِهِمْ إِنَّا
بُرَءَٰٓؤُا۟ مِنكُمْ وَمِمَّا تَعْبُدُونَ مِن دُونِ ٱللَّهِ كَفَرْنَا بِكُمْ وَبَدَا بَيْنَنَا وَبَيْنَكُمُ
ٱلْعَدَٰوَةُ وَٱلْبَغْضَآءُ أَبَدًا حَتَّىٰ تُؤْمِنُوا۟ بِٱللَّهِ وَحْدَهُۥٓ إِلَّا قَوْلَ إِبْرَٰهِيمَ لِأَبِيهِ
لَأَسْتَغْفِرَنَّ لَكَ وَمَآ أَمْلِكُ لَكَ مِنَ ٱللَّهِ مِن شَىْءٍ رَّبَّنَا عَلَيْكَ تَوَكَّلْنَا وَإِلَيْكَ
أَنَبْنَا وَإِلَيْكَ ٱلْمَصِيرُ ۝

There is for you an excellent example (to follow) in Abraham
and those with him, when they said to their people: "We
are clear of you and of whatever you worship besides Allah:
we have rejected you, and there has arisen, between us and
you, enmity and hatred forever – unless you believe in Allah
and Him alone": but not when Abraham said to his father:
"I will pray for forgiveness for you, though I have no power
(to get) aught on your behalf from Allah." (They prayed):
"Our Lord! In You do we trust, and to You do we turn in
repentance: to You is (our) final Goal."

al-Mumtaḥinah 60:4

These statements clearly establish that Ibrāhīm's audience was not ignorant of Allah's essence. Nor did they lack the understanding of His being *Rabb al-ʿālamīn*; they indeed worshipped God but associated others with Allah in His divinity. Hence why, in the Qur'ān, we do not find Ibrāhīm convincing his people to believe in Allah's person as *Ilāh* and *Rabb*. Rather, all he says is that Allah alone is the *Rabb* and the *Ilāh*.

Now take the case of Nimrūd. The Qur'ān reports his conversation with the Prophet Ibrāhīm in the following way:

أَلَمْ تَرَ إِلَى ٱلَّذِى حَآجَّ إِبْرَٰهِـمَ فِى رَبِّهِۦٓ أَنْ ءَاتَىٰهُ ٱللَّهُ ٱلْمُلْكَ إِذْ قَالَ إِبْرَٰهِـمُ رَبِّىَ ٱلَّذِى يُحْىِۦ وَيُمِيتُ قَالَ أَنَا۠ أُحْىِۦ وَأُمِيتُ ۖ قَالَ إِبْرَٰهِـمُ فَإِنَّ ٱللَّهَ يَأْتِى بِٱلشَّمْسِ مِنَ ٱلْمَشْرِقِ فَأْتِ بِهَا مِنَ ٱلْمَغْرِبِ فَبُهِتَ ٱلَّذِى كَفَرَ ۗ وَٱللَّهُ لَا يَهْدِى ٱلْقَوْمَ ٱلظَّـٰلِمِينَ ۝

Have you not turned your vision to one who disputed with Abraham about his Lord, because Allah had granted him power? Abraham said: "My Lord is He Who gives life and death." He said: "I give life and death." Said Abraham: "But it is Allah that causes the sun to rise from the East: do you then cause it to rise from the West?" Thus was he confounded who (in arrogance) rejected faith. Nor does Allah give guidance to a people unjust.

al-Baqarah 2:258

Clear as the conversation is, the dispute was not about the presence or non-presence of Allah but instead about Ibrāhīm's *Rabb*. There are two reasons for this. First, Nimrūd belonged to a stock of people who already acknowledged Allah's existence. Second, intelligent though he was, he knew he could not himself pose as the Creator of the earth and the heavens, nor did he believe that he was the cause for the sun-moon revolutions. For sure, he had no such claim to divinity nor had he entertained any thought of owning the heavens and the earth. Instead, his claim was *Rabb* specific – that he was the master and controller of his kingdom, which had, among others, Ibrāhīm as its subject. Even this claim did not fall within the first and second meanings of the word *Rabb*, for he believed in the divinity of the celestial bodies, and their ability to hurt or benefit humans. However, he qualified himself as the master – the god – of his kingdom because he considered everyone as his bonded subject, who had their collectivity and laws to live by because of his centrality and power. His words *"an ātāhul-Lāhu al-Mulk"* (whom Allah had granted power) identify his god complex, which stemmed from his perception about his imperial powers. Thus, when he came to know that a youth named Ibrāhīm was not only negating the divinity of the celestial bodies but also denying his political and socio-economic god trappings, he was upset. "Whom do you believe as your God?" Nimrūd asked Ibrāhīm. "One who has power to cause life and death," Ibrāhīm replied.

Inebriated as Nimrūd was with power, Ibrāhīm's answer hardly sunk into his skull. He made a similar claim to cause life and death for anyone he so chose. Countering him, Ibrāhīm (*'alayhis-salām*) said he believed in Allah as his God, Who alone qualified as the *Rabb*. Furthermore, there was no allowance for someone else's divinity, for such a person could not affect the phenomena of the sun's rising and setting. Intelligent as he was, Nimrūd got the drift. He knew for a fact that in Allah's kingdom his claim to divinity was a mere pretension. And this made him silent. His egotism and dynastic considerations, nevertheless, stifled any urge in him to surrender his unbounded authoritarianism and accept Allah and His messenger as his life's axle. Hence why, after reporting his speech, the Qur'ān says: *Wal-Lāhu lā yahdī al-qawm al-ẓālimīn* – but Allah does not guide the exceeders. Meaning thereby that after having known the message and still declining it, Nimrūd left Allah no choice but to ditch him as it is not Allah's way to impose guidance on those who have no desire for it.

Lūṭ's people

Following on the heels of Ibrāhīm's people came another nation scheduled for guidance by the Prophet Lūṭ (the biblical Lot), Ibrāhīm's nephew.

The Qur'ān tells us that these people too were neither the deniers of Allah's presence nor did they oppose His being the Provider and Nourisher of His creation. They did, however, refuse to accept Allah as their Master and Lawgiver. All they wanted was to be able to act on their own whimsical dictates – a capital crime that qualified them for punishment. The Qur'ān explains it as follows:

إِذْ قَالَ لَهُمْ أَخُوهُمْ لُوطٌ أَلَا تَتَّقُونَ ۞ إِنِّى لَكُمْ رَسُولٌ أَمِينٌ ۞ فَٱتَّقُوا اللَّهَ وَأَطِيعُونِ ۞ وَمَا أَسْـَٔلُكُمْ عَلَيْهِ مِنْ أَجْرٍ إِنْ أَجْرِىَ إِلَّا عَلَىٰ رَبِّ ٱلْعَـٰلَمِينَ ۞ أَتَأْتُونَ ٱلذُّكْرَانَ مِنَ ٱلْعَـٰلَمِينَ ۞ وَتَذَرُونَ مَا خَلَقَ لَكُمْ رَبُّكُم مِّنْ أَزْوَٰجِكُم بَلْ أَنتُمْ قَوْمٌ عَادُونَ ۞

Behold, their brother Lūṭ said to them: "Will you not fear (Allah)? I am to you a messenger worthy of all trust. So fear Allah and obey me. No reward do I ask of you for it: my reward is only from the Lord of the Worlds. Of all the creatures in the world, will you approach males, and leave those whom Allah has created for you to be your mates? No, you are a people transgressing (all limits)!"

al-Shuʿarāʾ 26:161-166

Lūṭ (*ʿalayhis-salām*) could only make such a speech to those who already believed in Allah's presence, His creativity and providence. Hence why their response did not question who Allah was. Nor did they question His creation of them or what made Him God. Instead, they said:

قَالُواْ لَبِن لَّمْ تَنتَهِ يَـٰلُوطُ لَتَكُونَنَّ مِنَ ٱلْمُخْرَجِينَ ۝

"If you desist not O Lūṭ! you will assuredly be cast out!"
al-Shuʿarāʾ 26:167

In another place, the Qurʾān describes the incident in a different way:

وَلُوطًا إِذْ قَالَ لِقَوْمِهِۦٓ إِنَّكُمْ لَتَأْتُونَ ٱلْفَـٰحِشَةَ مَا سَبَقَكُم بِهَا مِنْ أَحَدٍ
مِّنَ ٱلْعَـٰلَمِينَ ۝ أَئِنَّكُمْ لَتَأْتُونَ ٱلرِّجَالَ وَتَقْطَعُونَ ٱلسَّبِيلَ وَتَأْتُونَ فِى
نَادِيكُمُ ٱلْمُنكَرَ فَمَا كَانَ جَوَابَ قَوْمِهِۦٓ إِلَّآ أَن قَالُواْ ٱئْتِنَا بِعَذَابِ ٱللَّهِ
إِن كُنتَ مِنَ ٱلصَّـٰدِقِينَ ۝

And (remember) Lūṭ: behold, he said to his people: "You
do commit lewdness, such as no people in Creation (ever)
committed before you. Do you indeed approach men, and
cut off the highway? – and practise wickedness (even) in your
councils?" But his people gave no answer but this: they said:
"Bring us the Wrath of Allah if you tell the truth."
al-ʿAnkabūt 29:28-29

Could this be the response of a people who denied Allah?
Obviously, their real crime was not that they denied divinity for they
believed in the supernatural character of Allah as their *Ilāh* and *Rabb*,
but in the realms of morals, cultural and societal affairs. In these
aspects of their lives they refused to obey Allah and abide by His laws
as enunciated by His messenger.

Shuʿayb's people

The Midian people, among whom the Prophet Shuʿayb (*ʿalayhis-
salām*) was raised up, provide us with yet another example. They
came from Abrahamic stock, which makes it difficult to believe that

they denied Allah's divinity and providence. As a people, they grew in Islam but later they became perverse in their beliefs. The Qur'ān even describes them as proclaiming themselves *mu'min* (believers). This explains why Shuʿayb exhorted them to act properly if they were indeed believers. His whole speech and the responses he received indicated that they believed in Allah's divinity, though they suffered from two deviationist notions. First, they had begun to elevate others to divinity besides Allah in the supernatural sense. Their worship was, thus, not specific to Allah alone.

Second, their concept of Allah's divinity was exclusive to ritual worship and had nothing to do with the existential aspects of humanity – in the socio-economic and political realms of authority. They said they were free from Divine guidance in running their affairs. The following Qur'ānic *āyahs* support this contention:

وَإِلَىٰ مَدْيَنَ أَخَاهُمْ شُعَيْبًا قَالَ يَٰقَوْمِ ٱعْبُدُواْ ٱللَّهَ مَا لَكُم مِّنْ إِلَٰهٍ غَيْرُهُ قَدْ جَآءَتْكُم بَيِّنَةٌ مِّن رَّبِّكُمْ فَأَوْفُواْ ٱلْكَيْلَ وَٱلْمِيزَانَ وَلَا تَبْخَسُواْ ٱلنَّاسَ أَشْيَآءَهُمْ وَلَا تُفْسِدُواْ فِى ٱلْأَرْضِ بَعْدَ إِصْلَٰحِهَا ذَٰلِكُمْ خَيْرٌ لَّكُمْ إِن كُنتُم مُّؤْمِنِينَ ۞ وَلَا تَقْعُدُواْ بِكُلِّ صِرَٰطٍ تُوعِدُونَ وَتَصُدُّونَ عَن سَبِيلِ ٱللَّهِ مَنْ ءَامَنَ بِهِۦ وَتَبْغُونَهَا عِوَجًا وَٱذْكُرُوٓاْ إِذْ كُنتُمْ قَلِيلًا فَكَثَّرَكُمْ وَٱنظُرُواْ كَيْفَ كَانَ عَٰقِبَةُ ٱلْمُفْسِدِينَ ۞ وَإِن كَانَ طَآئِفَةٌ مِّنكُمْ ءَامَنُواْ بِٱلَّذِىٓ أُرْسِلْتُ بِهِۦ وَطَآئِفَةٌ لَّمْ يُؤْمِنُواْ فَٱصْبِرُواْ حَتَّىٰ يَحْكُمَ ٱللَّهُ بَيْنَنَا وَهُوَ خَيْرُ ٱلْحَٰكِمِينَ ۞

To the Madyan people We sent Shuʿayb, one of their own brethren: he said: "O my people! Worship Allah; you have no other god but Him. Now has come unto you a clear (Sign) from your Lord! Give just measure and weight, nor withhold from the people the things that are their due; and do no mischief on the earth after it has been set in order: that will be best for you, if you have faith. And squat not on every road, breathing threats, hindering from the path of Allah those who believe in Him, and seeking in it something crooked; but remember how you were little, and He gave you increase. And hold in your mind's eye what was the end of those who did mischief. And if there is a party among you who believes in the Message with which I have been sent, and a party which does not believe, hold yourselves in patience until Allah does decide between us: for He is the best to decide."

al-A'rāf 7:85-87

وَيَٰقَوۡمِ أَوۡفُواْ ٱلۡمِكۡيَالَ وَٱلۡمِيزَانَ بِٱلۡقِسۡطِۖ وَلَا تَبۡخَسُواْ ٱلنَّاسَ أَشۡيَاءَهُمۡ وَلَا تَعۡثَوۡاْ فِى ٱلۡأَرۡضِ مُفۡسِدِينَ ۝ بَقِيَّتُ ٱللَّهِ خَيۡرٌ لَّكُمۡ إِن كُنتُم مُّؤۡمِنِينَۚ وَمَآ أَنَا۠ عَلَيۡكُم بِحَفِيظٍ ۝ قَالُواْ يَٰشُعَيۡبُ أَصَلَوٰتُكَ تَأۡمُرُكَ أَن نَّتۡرُكَ مَا يَعۡبُدُ ءَابَآؤُنَآ أَوۡ أَن نَّفۡعَلَ فِىٓ أَمۡوَٰلِنَا مَا نَشَٰٓؤُاْۖ إِنَّكَ لَأَنتَ ٱلۡحَلِيمُ ٱلرَّشِيدُ ۝

"And O my people! Give just measure and weight, nor withhold from the people the things that are their due: commit not evil in the land with intent to do mischief. That which is left you by Allah is best for you, if you (but) believed! But I am not set over you to keep watch!" They said: "O Shu'ayb! Does your (religion of) prayer command you that we leave off the worship which our fathers practised, or that we leave off doing what we like with our property? Truly, you are the one that forbears with faults and is right-minded!"

Hūd 11:85-87

The summation of this *āyah* clearly indicates their perverse thinking about divinity.

Pharaoh and his people

Even greater misunderstanding about Pharaoh and his people exists. A common misperception about him is that he not only denied God but also promoted himself to the rank of Allah. In other words, he had gone insane, proclaiming before the world that he held the dominion of the earth and the heaven in his hands; and second, that his people were idiot enough to believe him. The Qur'ān and history give evidence to the contrary. In essence, Pharaoh's perversity was no different than Nimrūd's nor was his nation's perversity dissimilar to that of previous peoples.

The only difference was that in Pharaoh's case the conflict between him and the Israelites was primarily political. This had created a nationalistic hardheadedness and a prejudicial mindset, impelling him to deny Allah's divinity and providence, though inside, in his heart, he might have acknowledged Allah, as is the case with today's atheists.

The facts are that when the Prophet Yūsuf (the biblical Joseph) ascended to power in Egypt, he devoted himself to Islam's spread. His efforts paid off and so lasting an imprint of Islam did he impact on Egypt that for centuries none could efface it. Although it is possible that not all the Egyptians embraced Allah's true faith it is at the same time inconceivable that they were ignorant of Allah's existence and His attribute of Master of the earth and the heavens. Because of Islam's spread the Egyptians also came to believe in the divine and numinous person of Allah in the supernatural sense: Allah as the God of all gods and the Master of all masters save those who preferred to disbelieve and associated partners with Him. It is possible that the Islamic influences continued to linger on late into the century that saw the coming of the Prophet Mūsā (the biblical Moses). This receives support from the speech of a Coptic chieftain in Pharaoh's court. When the latter expressed his desire to kill Moses, the Coptic who had concealed his Islamic faith spoke out:

وَقَالَ رَجُلٌ مُّؤْمِنٌ مِّنْ ءَالِ فِرْعَوْنَ يَكْتُمُ إِيمَـٰنَهُۥٓ أَتَقْتُلُونَ رَجُلًا أَن يَقُولَ رَبِّىَ ٱللَّهُ وَقَدْ جَآءَكُم بِٱلْبَيِّنَـٰتِ مِن رَّبِّكُمْ وَإِن يَكُ كَـٰذِبًا فَعَلَيْهِ كَذِبُهُۥ وَإِن يَكُ صَادِقًا يُصِبْكُم بَعْضُ ٱلَّذِى يَعِدُكُمْ إِنَّ ٱللَّهَ لَا يَهْدِى مَنْ هُوَ مُسْرِفٌ كَذَّابٌ ۝ يَـٰقَوْمِ لَكُمُ ٱلْمُلْكُ ٱلْيَوْمَ ظَـٰهِرِينَ فِى ٱلْأَرْضِ فَمَن يَنصُرُنَا مِنۢ بَأْسِ ٱللَّهِ إِن جَآءَنَا قَالَ فِرْعَوْنُ مَآ أُرِيكُمْ إِلَّا مَآ أَرَىٰ وَمَآ أَهْدِيكُمْ إِلَّا سَبِيلَ ٱلرَّشَادِ ۝ وَقَالَ ٱلَّذِىٓ ءَامَنَ يَـٰقَوْمِ إِنِّىٓ أَخَافُ عَلَيْكُم مِّثْلَ يَوْمِ ٱلْأَحْزَابِ ۝ مِثْلَ دَأْبِ قَوْمِ نُوحٍ وَعَادٍ وَثَمُودَ وَٱلَّذِينَ مِنۢ بَعْدِهِمْ وَمَا ٱللَّهُ يُرِيدُ ظُلْمًا لِّلْعِبَادِ ۝ وَيَـٰقَوْمِ إِنِّىٓ أَخَافُ عَلَيْكُمْ يَوْمَ ٱلتَّنَادِ ۝ يَوْمَ تُوَلُّونَ مُدْبِرِينَ مَا لَكُم مِّنَ ٱللَّهِ مِنْ عَاصِمٍ وَمَن يُضْلِلِ ٱللَّهُ فَمَا لَهُۥ مِنْ هَادٍ ۝ وَلَقَدْ جَآءَكُمْ يُوسُفُ مِن قَبْلُ بِٱلْبَيِّنَـٰتِ فَمَا زِلْتُمْ فِى شَكٍّ مِّمَّا جَآءَكُم بِهِۦ حَتَّىٰٓ إِذَا هَلَكَ قُلْتُمْ لَن يَبْعَثَ ٱللَّهُ مِنۢ بَعْدِهِۦ رَسُولًا كَذَٰلِكَ يُضِلُّ ٱللَّهُ مَنْ هُوَ مُسْرِفٌ مُّرْتَابٌ ۝ ٱلَّذِينَ يُجَـٰدِلُونَ فِىٓ ءَايَـٰتِ ٱللَّهِ بِغَيْرِ سُلْطَـٰنٍ أَتَىٰهُمْ كَبُرَ مَقْتًا عِندَ ٱللَّهِ وَعِندَ ٱلَّذِينَ ءَامَنُوا۟ كَذَٰلِكَ يَطْبَعُ ٱللَّهُ عَلَىٰ كُلِّ قَلْبِ مُتَكَبِّرٍ جَبَّارٍ ۝ وَقَالَ فِرْعَوْنُ يَـٰهَـٰمَـٰنُ ٱبْنِ لِى صَرْحًا لَّعَلِّىٓ أَبْلُغُ ٱلْأَسْبَـٰبَ ۝ أَسْبَـٰبَ ٱلسَّمَـٰوَٰتِ فَأَطَّلِعَ إِلَىٰٓ إِلَـٰهِ مُوسَىٰ وَإِنِّى لَأَظُنُّهُۥ كَـٰذِبًا وَكَذَٰلِكَ زُيِّنَ لِفِرْعَوْنَ سُوٓءُ عَمَلِهِۦ وَصُدَّ عَنِ ٱلسَّبِيلِ وَمَا كَيْدُ فِرْعَوْنَ إِلَّا فِى تَبَابٍ ۝ وَقَالَ ٱلَّذِىٓ ءَامَنَ يَـٰقَوْمِ ٱتَّبِعُونِ أَهْدِكُمْ سَبِيلَ ٱلرَّشَادِ ۝ يَـٰقَوْمِ إِنَّمَا هَـٰذِهِ ٱلْحَيَوٰةُ ٱلدُّنْيَا مَتَـٰعٌ وَإِنَّ ٱلْءَاخِرَةَ هِىَ دَارُ ٱلْقَرَارِ ۝ مَنْ عَمِلَ سَيِّئَةً فَلَا يُجْزَىٰٓ إِلَّا مِثْلَهَا وَمَنْ عَمِلَ صَـٰلِحًا مِّن ذَكَرٍ أَوْ أُنثَىٰ وَهُوَ مُؤْمِنٌ فَأُو۟لَـٰٓئِكَ يَدْخُلُونَ

ٱلْجَنَّةَ يُرْزَقُونَ فِيهَا بِغَيْرِ حِسَابٍ ۞ وَيَٰقَوْمِ مَا لِىٓ أَدْعُوكُمْ إِلَى ٱلنَّجَوٰةِ
وَتَدْعُونَنِىٓ إِلَى ٱلنَّارِ ۞ تَدْعُونَنِى لِأَكْفُرَ بِٱللَّهِ وَأُشْرِكَ بِهِۦ مَا لَيْسَ لِى بِهِۦ
عِلْمٌ وَأَنَا۠ أَدْعُوكُمْ إِلَى ٱلْعَزِيزِ ٱلْغَفَّٰرِ ۞

A Believer, a man from among the people of Pharaoh, who had concealed his faith, said: "Will you slay a man because he says, 'My Lord is Allah'? when he has indeed come to you with clear (Signs) from your Lord? And if he be a liar, on him is (the sin of) his lie; but, if he is telling the Truth, then will fall on you something of the (calamity) of which he warns you: truly Allah guides not one who transgresses and lies! O my people! Yours is the dominion this day: you have the upper hand in the land: but who will help us from the punishment of Allah, should it befall us?" Pharaoh said: "I but point out to you that which I see (myself); nor do I guide you but to the right path!" Then said the man who believed: "O my people! Truly I do fear for you something like the Day (of disaster) of the Confederates (in sin)! Something like the fate of the people of Noah, the ʿĀd, and the Thamūd, and those who came after them: but Allah never wishes injustice to His servants. And O my people, I fear for you a Day when there will be mutual calling (and wailing) – a Day when you shall turn your backs and flee: no defender shall you have from Allah: any whom Allah leaves to stray, there is none to guide … And to you there came Joseph in times gone by, with clear Signs, but you ceased not to doubt of the (mission) for which he had come: at length, when he died, you said: 'No Messenger will Allah send after him.' Thus does Allah leave to stray such as transgress and live in doubt. (Such) as dispute about the Signs of Allah, without any authority that has reached them. Grievous and odious (is such conduct) in the sight of Allah and of the Believers. Thus does Allah seal up every heart – of arrogant and obstinate transgressors."

Pharaoh said: "O Hāmān! Build me a lofty palace, that I may attain the ways and means – the ways and means of (reaching) the heavens, and that I may mount up to the God of Moses: but as far as I am concerned, I think (Moses) is a liar!" Thus was made alluring, in Pharaoh's eyes the evil of his deeds, and he was hindered from the Path; and the plot of Pharaoh led to nothing but perdition (for him). The man who believed said further: "O my people! Follow me: I will lead you to the Path of Right. O my people! This life of the present is nothing but (temporary) convenience: it is the Hereafter that is the Home that will last. He that works evil will not be requited but by the like thereof: and he that works a righteous deed – whether man or woman – and is a Believer – such will enter the Garden (of Bliss): therein will they have abundance without measure. And O my people! How (strange) it is for me to call you to Salvation while you call me to the Fire! You do call upon me to blaspheme against Allah, and to join with Him partners of whom I have no knowledge; and I call you to the Exalted in Power, Who forgives again and again!"

al-Mu'min 40:28-42

This whole speech demonstrates that the impact of the Prophet Yūsuf's work had endured long after his death. So much so that when the conflict between Moses and Pharaoh was triggered, the Egyptians knew Allah and His attributes; they also knew that Allah was the *Rabb* and the *Ilāh*, that He prevailed over everything in nature, and that His wrath was fearsome. From the preceding *āyah* we also know that the Egyptians did not deny Allah's divinity and His power to sustain His creation. In essence, their deviation was no different from other peoples described in the Qur'ān – that is, they associated humans with Allah in terms of divinity and power.

Doubt does, however, arise in Pharaoh's mind when he hears the Prophet Moses say "*innā rasūlu Rabbi'l-'ālamīn* – we are the messenger from the God Who is the Master of all the universe". He, therefore, then asks "*wa mā Rabbu'l-'ālamīn* – and what is this Lord and Cherisher of the Worlds [you talk about]?" (*al-Shu'arā'* 26:23.)

He directs his minister Hāmān to build for him a tower high enough so that he can see the God of Moses. He threatens Moses with incarceration if the latter ever thought of making a god beside him. He also declares nationwide that he is their supreme lord, and that he knows of no other God beside himself. Utterances like these give one the impression that Pharaoh denied God's existence, that he had no concept of a God, Who was the Master of all the universes. The fact, however, is that his proclamations were the product of a nationalistic mindset. He was aware of the Prophet Yūsuf's influence as a *dā'iyah* and a ruler in spreading Islam in Egypt, which gave the Israelites much clout in society. For more than 300 years, the Israelites had held sway over Egypt, which eventually invited a backlash from the Egyptians in the form of a militant nationalism bringing in its fold a hardheaded nationalistic dynastic power.

So aggressive was this dynasty that it not only oppressed the Israelites but also set itself the task of wiping out the remnants of the prophetic era and reviving the old *jāhilī* religion. Thus, when Moses came, they felt that power might slip from their hands and see the Israelites once again enthroned. Again, it is because of this time-old animosity and hardheadedness that Pharaoh asks Moses tauntingly who this *Rabb al-'ālamīn* is that he talks about? Who can also be God beside him – Pharaoh? In fact, he knows well the *Ilāh* Who hold the keys to the heavens and the earth. His conversations with the Prophet Moses and the latter's speeches as reported in the Qur'ān confirm it. For instance, to assure his people about Moses' non-prophetic status, Pharaoh says:

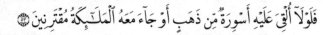

"Then why are not gold bracelets bestowed on him, or (why) come (not) with him angels accompanying him in procession?"

al-Zukhruf 43:53

Could a person not conversant with the notions of the prophetic office and angels say this? On another occasion, the following conversation takes place between Moses and Pharaoh:

وَلَقَدْ ءَاتَيْنَا مُوسَىٰ تِسْعَ ءَايَـٰتٍ بَيِّنَـٰتٍ فَسْـَٔلْ بَنِىٓ إِسْرَٰٓءِيلَ إِذْ جَآءَهُمْ
فَقَالَ لَهُۥ فِرْعَوْنُ إِنِّى لَأَظُنُّكَ يَـٰمُوسَىٰ مَسْحُورًا ۝ قَالَ لَقَدْ عَلِمْتَ
مَآ أَنزَلَ هَـٰٓؤُلَآءِ إِلَّا رَبُّ ٱلسَّمَـٰوَٰتِ وَٱلْأَرْضِ بَصَآئِرَ وَإِنِّى لَأَظُنُّكَ
يَـٰفِرْعَوْنُ مَثْبُورًا ۝

To Moses We did give nine clear Signs: ask the Children of Israel: when he came to them, Pharaoh said to him: "O Moses! I consider you, indeed, to have been worked upon by sorcery!" Moses said, "You know well that these things have been sent down by none but the Lord of the heavens and the earth as eye-opening evidence: and I consider you indeed, O Pharaoh, to be one doomed to destruction!"

al-Isrā' 17:101–102

On yet another occasion, Allah describes Pharaoh's psychological state in the following words:

فَلَمَّا جَآءَتْهُمْ ءَايَـٰتُنَا مُبْصِرَةً قَالُوا۟ هَـٰذَا سِحْرٌ مُّبِينٌ ۝ وَجَحَدُوا۟ بِهَا
وَٱسْتَيْقَنَتْهَآ أَنفُسُهُمْ ظُلْمًا وَعُلُوًّا فَٱنظُرْ كَيْفَ كَانَ عَـٰقِبَةُ ٱلْمُفْسِدِينَ ۝

But when Our Signs came to them that should have opened their eyes, they said: "This is sorcery manifest!" And they rejected those Signs in iniquity and arrogance, though their souls were convinced thereof: so see what was the end of those who acted corruptly!

al-Naml 27:13–14

Furthermore, the Qur'ān describes one of their meetings as follows:

قَالَ لَهُم مُّوسَىٰ وَيْلَكُمْ لَا تَفْتَرُواْ عَلَى ٱللَّهِ كَذِبًا فَيُسْحِتَكُم بِعَذَابٍ وَقَدْ خَابَ مَنِ ٱفْتَرَىٰ ۞ فَتَنَـٰزَعُوٓاْ أَمْرَهُم بَيْنَهُمْ وَأَسَرُّواْ ٱلنَّجْوَىٰ ۞ قَالُوٓاْ إِنْ هَـٰذَٰنِ لَسَـٰحِرَٰنِ يُرِيدَانِ أَن يُخْرِجَاكُم مِّنْ أَرْضِكُم بِسِحْرِهِمَا وَيَذْهَبَا بِطَرِيقَتِكُمُ ٱلْمُثْلَىٰ ۞

Moses said to them: "Woe to you! Forge not you a lie against Allah, lest He destroy you (at once) utterly by chastisement: the forger must suffer frustration!" So they disputed, one with another, over their affair, but they kept their talk secret. They said: "These two are certainly (expert) magicians: their object is to drive you out from your land with their magic, and to do away with your most cherished institutions."

Ṭā Hā 20:61-63

Obviously, Moses' allusion to Divine retribution in response to their linking falsehood with Allah provoked soul searching in them for they still possessed their fear of Allah. But before they could amend their thinking, members of their nationalistic ruling élite scared them away by invoking the spectre of a political change engineered by Moses and Aaron. At the thought of a return to Israelite supremacy their hearts lost their receptivity to Moses, and, thus, their decision to resist the prophetic call was inevitable.

The situation thus clarified, we can now easily probe the nature of the conflict between Moses and Pharaoh. We can also identify the thrust, import and perversion behind Pharaoh's claim to divinity and lordship:

وَقَالَ ٱلْمَلَأُ مِن قَوْمِ فِرْعَوْنَ أَتَذَرُ مُوسَىٰ وَقَوْمَهُۥ لِيُفْسِدُواْ فِى ٱلْأَرْضِ
وَيَذَرَكَ وَءَالِهَتَكَ قَالَ سَنُقَتِّلُ أَبْنَآءَهُمْ وَنَسْتَحْىِۦ نِسَآءَهُمْ وَإِنَّا فَوْقَهُمْ
قَٰهِرُونَ ۝

Said the chiefs of the Pharaoh people: "Will you leave Moses
and his people to spread mischief in the land, and to abandon
you and your gods?" He said: "Their male children will we
slay; (only) their females will we save alive; and we have over
them (power) irresistible."

al-A'rāf 7:127

In response to this, a person in Pharaoh's court who had embraced
Moses' faith spoke to these people as follows:

تَدْعُونَنِى لِأَكْفُرَ بِٱللَّهِ وَأُشْرِكَ بِهِۦ مَا لَيْسَ لِى بِهِۦ عِلْمٌ وَأَنَا۠ أَدْعُوكُمْ إِلَى
ٱلْعَزِيزِ ٱلْغَفَّٰرِ ۝

"You do call upon me to blaspheme against Allah, and to
join with Him partners of whom I have no knowledge; and
I call you to the Exalted in Power, Who forgives again and
again!"

al-Mu'min 40:42

When we combine these two *āyahs* with the information thrown
up by history and archaeology relating to the Egyptians of Pharaoh's
time, we know for a fact that they anthropomorphized elements of
nature into godhead and associated these with Allah. Obviously, if
Pharaoh had been a claimant to divinity in the supernatural sense –
that is, if he had proclaimed himself to have control over the causative
factors in the universe - he would not have worshipped other gods.

The Qur'ān reproduces Pharaoh's words thus:

وَقَالَ فِرْعَوْنُ يَـٰٓأَيُّهَا ٱلْمَلَأُ مَا عَلِمْتُ لَكُم مِّنْ إِلَـٰهٍ غَيْرِى فَأَوْقِدْ لِى يَـٰهَـٰمَـٰنُ عَلَى ٱلطِّينِ فَٱجْعَل لِّى صَرْحًا لَّعَلِّىٓ أَطَّلِعُ إِلَىٰٓ إِلَـٰهِ مُوسَىٰ وَإِنِّى لَأَظُنُّهُۥ مِنَ ٱلْكَـٰذِبِينَ ۝

Pharaoh said: "O Chiefs! No god do I know for you but myself: therefore, O Hāmān! light me a (kiln to bake bricks) out of clay, and build me a lofty palace, that I may mount up to the god of Moses: but as far as I am concerned, I think Moses is a liar!"

al-Qaṣaṣ 28:38

قَالَ لَئِنِ ٱتَّخَذْتَ إِلَـٰهًا غَيْرِى لَأَجْعَلَنَّكَ مِنَ ٱلْمَسْجُونِينَ ۝

(Pharaoh) said: "If you do put forward any god other than me, I will certainly put you in prison!"

al-Shuʿarā' 26:29

The preceding *āyahs* do not imply that Pharaoh negated every other god but himself. Rather, he sought to refute Moses' invitation to the truth, for the latter was calling them to an *Ilāh* Who was not only supernatural but also the Issuer of command in a political and civilizational context. Thus to counter him, Pharaoh said to his nation that it should have no god but him. At the same time, he threatened Moses with dire consequences if he continued to take someone else as god in the sense of a lawgiver and sovereign.

The Qur'ānic *āyahs* also suggest, supported by history and archaeology, that the Egyptian pharaohs not only proclaimed themselves to hold sovereignty but also claimed holiness in order to retain their hold on the masses. In many parts of the world, dynastic rule has ascribed supernatural status to itself, claiming that it is invested with divinity and, hence, should be worshipped by others. That others should worship such rulers is an adjunct to their political domination for which they use divinity as a prop. This helps explain why with the diminution of their political influence dynastic families lost their hallowed supernatural face as well, though perhaps not unexpectedly this was then acquired by the new entrants to power.

Pharaoh's real claim was not to supernatural divinity but political absolutism. He said loud and clear that he alone was the overlord of the Egyptian people, that he was the possessor of all material and human resources, that he alone had the right to absolute control and power, that he was the civilizational pivot and the hub of every aspect of collective life, and that his word was law to the exclusion of all else. The Qur'ān couches Pharoah's claim in the following *āyah*:

$$\text{وَنَادَىٰ فِرْعَوْنُ فِى قَوْمِهِ قَالَ يَـٰقَوْمِ أَلَيْسَ لِى مُلْكُ مِصْرَ وَهَـٰذِهِ ٱلْأَنْهَـٰرُ تَجْرِى مِن تَحْتِىٓ أَفَلَا تُبْصِرُونَ ۞}$$

And Pharaoh proclaimed among his people, saying: "O my people! Does not the dominion of Egypt belong to me; (witness) these streams flowing underneath my (palace)? What! See you not then?"

al-Zukhruf 43:51

This was the same basis upon which Nimrūd rested his claim to providence – *ḥājja Ibrāhīma fī Rabbihi an ātāhul-Lāhu al-mulk*. (The one who disputed with Abraham about his Lord because Allah had granted him power) Yūsuf's contemporary, the Egyptian king, had also arrogated to himself the role of lord and master of his people.

The contentious point between Moses and Pharaoh was none other than Allah's status as the only God, the Master of the universe as well as the focal point of political and social behaviour. To Moses, it was Allah alone Who held these aspects of power in the supernatural sense.

Elaborating upon the implications of power, Moses told Pharaoh that worship was for Allah only and so was obedience. It was His law that called for compliance. Besides, Allah had appointed him as His representative, and through him gave His commandments. Thus, the right to rule over His people was vested in him. Forthright as his speech was, it explained why Pharaoh and his functionaries repeatedly said that these two brothers (Moses and Aaron) wanted to dispossess them and obtain dominion over Egypt so that they could replace the Egyptian religion and way of life with theirs.

وَلَقَدْ أَرْسَلْنَا مُوسَىٰ بِـَٔايَٰتِنَا وَسُلْطَٰنٍ مُّبِينٍ ۞ إِلَىٰ فِرْعَوْنَ وَمَلَإِيْهِ فَٱتَّبَعُوٓاْ أَمْرَ فِرْعَوْنَ وَمَآ أَمْرُ فِرْعَوْنَ بِرَشِيدٍ ۞

And We sent Moses with Our clear (Signs) and an authority manifest unto Pharaoh and his Chiefs: but they followed the command of Pharaoh, and the command of Pharaoh was no right (guide).

Hūd 11:96-97

۞ وَلَقَدْ فَتَنَّا قَبْلَهُمْ قَوْمَ فِرْعَوْنَ وَجَآءَهُمْ رَسُولٌ كَرِيمٌ ۞ أَنْ أَدُّوٓاْ إِلَىَّ عِبَادَ ٱللَّهِ إِنِّى لَكُمْ رَسُولٌ أَمِينٌ ۞ وَأَن لَّا تَعْلُواْ عَلَى ٱللَّهِ إِنِّىٓ ءَاتِيكُم بِسُلْطَٰنٍ مُّبِينٍ ۞

We did, before them, try the people of Pharaoh: there came to them a messenger most honourable, saying: "Restore to me the servants of Allah: I am to you a messenger worthy of all trust; and be not arrogant as against Allah: for I come to you with authority manifest."

al-Dukhān 44:17-19

إِنَّآ أَرْسَلْنَآ إِلَيْكُمْ رَسُولًا شَٰهِدًا عَلَيْكُمْ كَمَآ أَرْسَلْنَآ إِلَىٰ فِرْعَوْنَ رَسُولًا ۝ فَعَصَىٰ فِرْعَوْنُ ٱلرَّسُولَ فَأَخَذْنَٰهُ أَخْذًا وَبِيلًا ۝

We have sent to you, (O men!) a messenger, to be a witness concerning you, even as We sent a messenger to Pharaoh. But Pharaoh disobeyed the messenger; so We seized him with a heavy Punishment.

al-Muzzammil 73:15-16

قَالَ فَمَن رَّبُّكُمَا يَٰمُوسَىٰ ۝ قَالَ رَبُّنَا ٱلَّذِىٓ أَعْطَىٰ كُلَّ شَىْءٍ خَلْقَهُۥ ثُمَّ هَدَىٰ ۝

(When this message was delivered), (Pharaoh) said: "Who then, O Moses, is the Lord of you two?" He said: "Our Lord is He Who gave to each (created) thing its form and nature, and further, gave (it) guidance."

Ṭā Hā 20:49-50

قَالَ فِرْعَوْنُ وَمَا رَبُّ ٱلْعَٰلَمِينَ ۝ قَالَ رَبُّ ٱلسَّمَٰوَٰتِ وَٱلْأَرْضِ وَمَا بَيْنَهُمَآ إِن كُنتُم مُّوقِنِينَ ۝ قَالَ لِمَنْ حَوْلَهُۥٓ أَلَا تَسْتَمِعُونَ ۝ قَالَ رَبُّكُمْ وَرَبُّ ءَابَآئِكُمُ ٱلْأَوَّلِينَ ۝ قَالَ إِنَّ رَسُولَكُمُ ٱلَّذِىٓ أُرْسِلَ إِلَيْكُمْ لَمَجْنُونٌ ۝ قَالَ رَبُّ ٱلْمَشْرِقِ وَٱلْمَغْرِبِ وَمَا بَيْنَهُمَآ إِن كُنتُمْ تَعْقِلُونَ ۝ قَالَ لَئِنِ ٱتَّخَذْتَ إِلَٰهًا غَيْرِى لَأَجْعَلَنَّكَ مِنَ ٱلْمَسْجُونِينَ ۝

Pharaoh said: "And what is the 'Lord and Cherisher of the Worlds'?" (Moses) said: "The Lord and Cherisher of the heavens and the earth, and all between – if you want to be quite sure." (Pharaoh) said to those around: "Do you not listen (to what he says)?" (Moses) said: "Your Lord and the Lord of your fathers from the beginning!" (Pharaoh) said: "Truly your messenger who has been sent to you is a veritable madman!" (Moses) said: "Lord of the East and the West, and all between! If you only had sense!" (Pharaoh) said: "If you serve any other god but me, I will certainly throw you in prison!"

al-Shuʿarāʾ 26:23-29

قَالَ أَجِئْتَنَا لِتُخْرِجَنَا مِنْ أَرْضِنَا بِسِحْرِكَ يَـٰمُوسَىٰ ۝

He said: "Have you come to drive us out of our land with your magic, O Moses?"

Ṭā Hā 20:57

وَقَالَ فِرْعَوْنُ ذَرُونِيٓ أَقْتُلْ مُوسَىٰ وَلْيَدْعُ رَبَّهُۥٓ إِنِّىٓ أَخَافُ أَن يُبَدِّلَ دِينَكُمْ أَوْ أَن يُظْهِرَ فِى ٱلْأَرْضِ ٱلْفَسَادَ ۝

Said Pharaoh: "Leave me to slay Moses; and let him call on his Lord! What I fear is lest he should change your religion, or lest he should cause mischief to appear in the land!"

al-Muʾmin 40:26

قَالُوٓاْ إِنْ هَـٰذَانِ لَسَـٰحِرَانِ يُرِيدَانِ أَن يُخْرِجَاكُم مِّنْ أَرْضِكُم بِسِحْرِهِمَا وَيَذْهَبَا بِطَرِيقَتِكُمُ ٱلْمُثْلَىٰ ۝

They said: "These two are certainly (expert) magicians: their object is to drive you out from your land with their magic, and to do away with your most cherished institutions."

Ṭā Hā 20:63

By arranging these *āyahs* together one gets the picture of the Egyptians' perversity: they suffered from the same disease that other nations had. Moses and Aaron were inviting them to the same message that the past prophets had given earlier nations, but in the same vein Egypt too proved no exception.

The Jews and the Christians

Like the peoples before them, the Israelites and those around them that accepted either Judaism or somewhat later Christianity demonstrated the same susceptibility. The Qur'ān calls them scriptural people, but it is difficult to think that they could have gone so far as to deny God's existence, or that they could have withheld recognition of God as their Deity and the Master of the universe. Yet that being the case, what exactly qualified them for the epithet deviant people? The Qur'ān provides the answer:

قُلْ يَـٰٓأَهْلَ ٱلْكِتَـٰبِ لَا تَغْلُوا۟ فِى دِينِكُمْ غَيْرَ ٱلْحَقِّ وَلَا تَتَّبِعُوٓا۟ أَهْوَآءَ
قَوْمٍ قَدْ ضَلُّوا۟ مِن قَبْلُ وَأَضَلُّوا۟ كَثِيرًا وَضَلُّوا۟ عَن سَوَآءِ ٱلسَّبِيلِ ۝

Say: "O People of the Book! Exceed not in your religion the
bounds (of what is proper), trespassing beyond the truth, nor
follow the vain desires of people who went wrong in times
gone by – who misled many, and strayed (themselves) from
the even Way."

al-Mā'idah 5:77

This demonstrates how both the Jews and Christians suffered from the same perversity that others did and which, as the Qur'ān tells us, came to them through their exaggerated attitudes toward religion. The Qur'ān describes this in the following words:

وَقَالَتِ ٱلْيَهُودُ عُزَيْرٌ ٱبْنُ ٱللَّهِ وَقَالَتِ ٱلنَّصَـٰرَى ٱلْمَسِيحُ ٱبْنُ ٱللَّهِ ذَٰلِكَ
قَوْلُهُم بِأَفْوَٰهِهِمْ يُضَـٰهِـُٔونَ قَوْلَ ٱلَّذِينَ كَفَرُوا۟ مِن قَبْلُ قَـٰتَلَهُمُ ٱللَّهُ
أَنَّىٰ يُؤْفَكُونَ ۝

The Jews call 'Uzayr a son of God, and the Christians call
Christ the Son of God. That is a saying from their mouth;
(in this) they but imitate what the unbelievers of old used

to say. Allah's curse be on them: how they are deluded away
from the Truth!

al-Tawbah 9:30

لَّقَدْ كَفَرَ ٱلَّذِينَ قَالُوٓاْ إِنَّ ٱللَّهَ هُوَ ٱلْمَسِيحُ ٱبْنُ مَرْيَمَ وَقَالَ ٱلْمَسِيحُ يَـٰبَنِىٓ
إِسْرَٰٓءِيلَ ٱعْبُدُواْ ٱللَّهَ رَبِّى وَرَبَّكُمْ إِنَّهُۥ مَن يُشْرِكْ بِٱللَّهِ فَقَدْ حَرَّمَ ٱللَّهُ عَلَيْهِ
ٱلْجَنَّةَ وَمَأْوَىٰهُ ٱلنَّارُ وَمَا لِلظَّـٰلِمِينَ مِنْ أَنصَارٍ ۞ لَّقَدْ كَفَرَ ٱلَّذِينَ قَالُوٓاْ إِنَّ
ٱللَّهَ ثَالِثُ ثَلَـٰثَةٍ وَمَا مِنْ إِلَـٰهٍ إِلَّآ إِلَـٰهٌ وَٰحِدٌ وَإِن لَّمْ يَنتَهُواْ عَمَّا يَقُولُونَ
لَيَمَسَّنَّ ٱلَّذِينَ كَفَرُواْ مِنْهُمْ عَذَابٌ أَلِيمٌ ۞

They do blaspheme who say: "Allah is Christ the son of
Mary." But said Christ: "O Children of Israel! Worship
Allah, my Lord and your Lord." Whoever joins other gods
with Allah – Allah will forbid him the Garden, and the Fire
will be his abode. There will for the wrongdoers be no one
to help. They do blaspheme who say: Allah is one of three in
a trinity: for there is no god except One God. If they desist
not from their word (of blasphemy), verily a grievous penalty
will befall the blasphemers among them.

al-Mā'idah 5:72-73

وَإِذْ قَالَ ٱللَّهُ يَـٰعِيسَى ٱبْنَ مَرْيَمَ ءَأَنتَ قُلْتَ لِلنَّاسِ ٱتَّخِذُونِى وَأُمِّىَ إِلَـٰهَيْنِ
مِن دُونِ ٱللَّهِ قَالَ سُبْحَـٰنَكَ مَا يَكُونُ لِىٓ أَنْ أَقُولَ مَا لَيْسَ لِى بِحَقٍّ إِن
كُنتُ قُلْتُهُۥ فَقَدْ عَلِمْتَهُۥ تَعْلَمُ مَا فِى نَفْسِى وَلَآ أَعْلَمُ مَا فِى نَفْسِكَ إِنَّكَ أَنتَ
عَلَّـٰمُ ٱلْغُيُوبِ ۞

Recall when Allah will say: "O Jesus, son of Maryam! Was it
you who said to the people: 'Take me and my mother as two
gods besides Allah?'" Jesus will say: "Glory be to You! It was
not for me to say that to which I had no right."

al-Mā'idah 5:116

مَا كَانَ لِبَشَرٍ أَن يُؤْتِيَهُ ٱللَّهُ ٱلْكِتَـٰبَ وَٱلْحُكْمَ وَٱلنُّبُوَّةَ ثُمَّ يَقُولَ لِلنَّاسِ
كُونُواْ عِبَادًا لِّى مِن دُونِ ٱللَّهِ وَلَـٰكِن كُونُواْ رَبَّـٰنِيِّـۧنَ بِمَا كُنتُمْ تُعَلِّمُونَ
ٱلْكِتَـٰبَ وَبِمَا كُنتُمْ تَدْرُسُونَ ۞ وَلَا يَأْمُرَكُمْ أَن تَتَّخِذُواْ ٱلْمَلَـٰئِكَةَ
وَٱلنَّبِيِّـۧنَ أَرْبَابًا أَيَأْمُرُكُم بِٱلْكُفْرِ بَعْدَ إِذْ أَنتُم مُّسْلِمُونَ ۞

It is not (possible) that a man, to whom is given the Book, and Wisdom, and the prophetic office, should say to people: "Be my worshippers rather than Allah's": on the contrary (he would say): "Be worshippers of Him Who is truly the Cherisher of all: for you have taught the Book and you have studied it earnestly." Nor would he instruct you to take angels and prophets for lords and patrons. What! Would he bid you to unbelief after you have bowed your will (to Allah in Islam)?

Āl 'Imrān 3:79-80

From the preceding *āyahs*, it is obvious that they had endowed their prophets and saints with godly attributes, making them partners with Allah in running the universe. They had dressed them up with supernaturalism and providence, seeking their help in need and safety from harm.

Furthermore, they imparted divinity to their clergy and religious leaders, allowing them to proscribe things for them:

ٱتَّخَذُواْ أَحْبَارَهُمْ وَرُهْبَـٰنَهُمْ أَرْبَابًا مِّن دُونِ ٱللَّهِ وَٱلْمَسِيحَ ٱبْنَ مَرْيَمَ
وَمَآ أُمِرُوٓاْ إِلَّا لِيَعْبُدُوٓاْ إِلَـٰهًا وَٰحِدًا لَّآ إِلَـٰهَ إِلَّا هُوَ سُبْحَـٰنَهُۥ
عَمَّا يُشْرِكُونَ ۞

They take their priests and their anchorites to be their lords in derogation of Allah, and (they take as their lord) Christ, the son of Mary: yet they were commanded to worship but One

God: there is no god but He. Praise and glory to Him: (far is
He) from having the partners they associate (with Him).

al-Tawbah 9:31

Expressed differently, they facilitated the metamorphosis of their
religious scholars into the arbitrary authority of God. They violated
their role of telling people to follow the *Sharī'ah* and of helping them
in their moral rehabilitation. In this way, they became infested with
the same primary diseases that marked Noah's people, Ibrāhīm's, the
'Ād, the Thamūd, the Madā'in and others. Like them, they ascribed
participatory divinity with Allah to angels and others. And like them,
they consigned civil and political suzerainty to humans instead of
Allah. In the process, they freed every aspect of human life from the
divine grid. Once that happened, their fall could only be imminent.
The Qur'ān says of this:

أَلَمْ تَرَ إِلَى ٱلَّذِينَ أُوتُواْ نَصِيبًا مِّنَ ٱلْكِتَـٰبِ يُؤْمِنُونَ بِٱلْجِبْتِ وَٱلطَّـٰغُوتِ
وَيَقُولُونَ لِلَّذِينَ كَفَرُواْ هَـٰٓؤُلَآءِ أَهْدَىٰ مِنَ ٱلَّذِينَ ءَامَنُواْ سَبِيلًا ۝

Have you not turned your vision to those who were given a
portion of the Book? They believe in sorcery and evil, and say
to the unbelievers that they are better guided in the (right)
way than the believers!

al-Nisā' 4:51

قُلْ هَلْ أُنَبِّئُكُم بِشَرٍّ مِّن ذَٰلِكَ مَثُوبَةً عِندَ ٱللَّهِ مَن لَّعَنَهُ ٱللَّهُ وَغَضِبَ عَلَيْهِ
وَجَعَلَ مِنْهُمُ ٱلْقِرَدَةَ وَٱلْخَنَازِيرَ وَعَبَدَ ٱلطَّـٰغُوتَ أُوْلَـٰٓئِكَ شَرٌّ مَّكَانًا
وَأَضَلُّ عَن سَوَآءِ ٱلسَّبِيلِ ۝

Say: "Shall I point out to you something much worse than
this, (as judged) by the treatment it received from Allah?
Those who incurred the curse of Allah and His wrath, those
of whom some He transformed into apes and swine, those

who worshipped evil – these are (many times) worse in rank,
and far more astray from the even path!"

al-Mā'idah 5:60

The word *jibt* used in these *āyah* is a cumulative expression that
entails all kinds of superstitions, including magic, occultation, zodiac
signs and their influences, and so forth. *Ṭāghūt*, another expression
used, implies any person, group or institution that has become
rebellious in the face of Allah's authority by ascribing divinity to
itself. The first ailment opened up the floodgates of superstition that
eventually overpowered them. The second, whilst elevating the rabbis,
priests, and pious ascetics to heights above their station, also delivered
both they and the people into the servitude of despots and tyrants who
hated everything and anything associated with God.

The Arabian polytheists

Now, we have to find out what kind of perversity the Qur'ān's first
audience – the Arabian polytheists – suffered from. Were they unaware
of God's existence? Or if they refuted Him, was the Prophet sent to
convince them of Allah's existence? Or if they denied Allah as God
and Master, was this the sole reason for the Qur'ān's revelation to
make them realize Allah's divinity and providence? Did they refuse
to worship Allah or did they deny His ability to listen and respond to
their needs? Did they take al-Lāt, al-Manāt, al-Hubal and al-ʿUzzā
and their likes as the real creators, masters and providents of the
universe? Did they consider their gods as the founts of guidance? To
each of these questions, the Qur'ān answers in the negative.

The Arabian polytheists not only believed in Allah's existence but
also considered Him as the Master of everything including their petty
gods. Hence, when all else failed, they called upon Him in distress.
They also did not refuse to worship Him. In fact, the Qur'ān tells
us that they neither took their gods as creators and providers of this
universe nor did they believe them to be the givers of guidance in
life matters.

قُل لِّمَنِ ٱلْأَرْضُ وَمَن فِيهَآ إِن كُنتُمْ تَعْلَمُونَ ۝ سَيَقُولُونَ لِلَّهِ قُلْ
أَفَلَا تَذَكَّرُونَ ۝ قُلْ مَن رَّبُّ ٱلسَّمَٰوَٰتِ ٱلسَّبْعِ وَرَبُّ ٱلْعَرْشِ
ٱلْعَظِيمِ ۝ سَيَقُولُونَ لِلَّهِ قُلْ أَفَلَا تَتَّقُونَ ۝ قُلْ مَنۢ بِيَدِهِۦ مَلَكُوتُ كُلِّ
شَىْءٍ وَهُوَ يُجِيرُ وَلَا يُجَارُ عَلَيْهِ إِن كُنتُمْ تَعْلَمُونَ ۝ سَيَقُولُونَ لِلَّهِ قُلْ فَأَنَّىٰ
تُسْحَرُونَ ۝ بَلْ أَتَيْنَٰهُم بِٱلْحَقِّ وَإِنَّهُمْ لَكَٰذِبُونَ ۝

Say: "To whom belong the earth and all beings therein?
(Say) if you know!" They will say, "To Allah!" Say: "Still,
will you not receive admonition?" Say: "Who is the Lord of
the seven heavens, and the Lord of the Throne (of Glory)
Supreme?" They will say, "(They belong) to Allah." Say:
"Will you not then be filled with awe?" Say: "Who is it in
whose hands is the governance of all things – Who protects
(all) but is not protected (by any)? (Say) if you know." They
will say, "(It belongs) to Allah," Say: "Then how are you
deluded?" We have sent them the Truth: but they indeed
practise falsehood!

al-Mu'minūn 23:84-90

هُوَ ٱلَّذِى يُسَيِّرُكُمْ فِى ٱلْبَرِّ وَٱلْبَحْرِ ۖ حَتَّىٰٓ إِذَا كُنتُمْ فِى ٱلْفُلْكِ وَجَرَيْنَ بِهِم
بِرِيحٍ طَيِّبَةٍ وَفَرِحُوا۟ بِهَا جَآءَتْهَا رِيحٌ عَاصِفٌ وَجَآءَهُمُ ٱلْمَوْجُ مِن كُلِّ
مَكَانٍ وَظَنُّوٓا۟ أَنَّهُمْ أُحِيطَ بِهِمْ ۙ دَعَوُا۟ ٱللَّهَ مُخْلِصِينَ لَهُ ٱلدِّينَ لَئِنْ أَنجَيْتَنَا مِنْ
هَٰذِهِۦ لَنَكُونَنَّ مِنَ ٱلشَّٰكِرِينَ ۝ فَلَمَّآ أَنجَىٰهُمْ إِذَا هُمْ يَبْغُونَ فِى ٱلْأَرْضِ
بِغَيْرِ ٱلْحَقِّ ۗ يَٰٓأَيُّهَا ٱلنَّاسُ إِنَّمَا بَغْيُكُمْ عَلَىٰٓ أَنفُسِكُم ۖ مَّتَٰعَ ٱلْحَيَوٰةِ ٱلدُّنْيَا ۖ ثُمَّ
إِلَيْنَا مَرْجِعُكُمْ فَنُنَبِّئُكُم بِمَا كُنتُمْ تَعْمَلُونَ ۝

He it is Who enabled you to traverse through land and sea;
so that you even board ships; they sail with them with a

favourable wind, and they rejoice thereat; then comes a
stormy wind and the waves come to them from all sides, and
they think they are being overwhelmed: they cry unto Him,
saying, "If You do deliver us from this, we shall truly show
our gratitude!" But when He delivers them, they transgress
insolently through the earth in defiance of right! O mankind!
Your insolence is against your own souls – an enjoyment of
the life of the present: in the end, to Us is your return, and
We shall show you the truth of all that you did.

Yūnus 10:22-23

وَإِذَا مَسَّكُمُ ٱلضُّرُّ فِى ٱلْبَحْرِ ضَلَّ مَن تَدْعُونَ إِلَّآ إِيَّاهُ فَلَمَّا نَجَّىٰكُمْ إِلَى
ٱلْبَرِّ أَعْرَضْتُمْ وَكَانَ ٱلْإِنسَـٰنُ كَفُورًا ۝

When distress seizes you at sea, those that you call upon
– besides Himself – leave you in the lurch! But when He
brings you back safe to land, you turn away (from Him).
Most ungrateful is man!

al-Isrā' 17:67

The Qur'ān tells us what they thought about their gods:

أَلَا لِلَّهِ ٱلدِّينُ ٱلْخَالِصُ وَٱلَّذِينَ ٱتَّخَذُوا۟ مِن دُونِهِۦٓ أَوْلِيَآءَ مَا نَعْبُدُهُمْ
إِلَّا لِيُقَرِّبُونَآ إِلَى ٱللَّهِ زُلْفَىٰٓ إِنَّ ٱللَّهَ يَحْكُمُ بَيْنَهُمْ فِى مَا هُمْ فِيهِ يَخْتَلِفُونَ إِنَّ
ٱللَّهَ لَا يَهْدِى مَنْ هُوَ كَـٰذِبٌ كَفَّارٌ ۝

To Allah alone is true worship due. As for those who choose
other guardians besides Him, (saying): "We serve them only
that they may bring us nearer to Allah," truly Allah will judge
between them in that wherein they differ. But Allah guides
not such as are false and ungrateful.

al-Zumar 39:3

وَيَعْبُدُونَ مِن دُونِ ٱللَّهِ مَا لَا يَضُرُّهُمْ وَلَا يَنفَعُهُمْ وَيَقُولُونَ هَٰٓؤُلَآءِ شُفَعَٰٓؤُنَا عِندَ ٱللَّهِ قُلْ أَتُنَبِّئُونَ ٱللَّهَ بِمَا لَا يَعْلَمُ فِى ٱلسَّمَٰوَٰتِ وَلَا فِى ٱلْأَرْضِ سُبْحَٰنَهُۥ وَتَعَٰلَىٰ عَمَّا يُشْرِكُونَ ۝

They serve, besides Allah, that which can neither harm nor help them, and say "These are our intercessors with Allah." Say: "Do you presume to tell Allah of something He knows not, in the heavens or on earth? Glory to Him! And far is He above the partners they ascribe (to Him)!"

Yūnus 10:18

Besides, they did not suffer under the delusion that their gods could give them guidance in matters of life. Thus, Allah enjoins on His Prophet to ask the non-believers:

قُلْ هَلْ مِن شُرَكَآئِكُم مَّن يَهْدِىٓ إِلَى ٱلْحَقِّ قُلِ ٱللَّهُ يَهْدِى لِلْحَقِّ أَفَمَن يَهْدِىٓ إِلَى ٱلْحَقِّ أَحَقُّ أَن يُتَّبَعَ أَمَّن لَّا يَهِدِّىٓ إِلَّآ أَن يُهْدَىٰ فَمَا لَكُمْ كَيْفَ تَحْكُمُونَ ۝

Say: "Of your 'partners' is there any that can give any guidance towards Truth?" Say: "It is Allah Who gives guidance towards Truth. Is then He Who gives guidance to Truth more worthy to be followed or he who finds not guidance (himself) unless he is guided? What then is the matter with you? How judge you?"

Yūnus 10:35

The question nevertheless silences them. None dared say that al-Lāt and al-Manāt gave life-specific instructions or that they taught the principles of justice and peace, and that because of their teachings some basics in the mysteries of the universe were learned. In the absence of such a response, Allah then asks His Prophet to say it is He alone Who gives guidance and none else.

Having explained their mindset, there is still one question left unanswered: what precisely was their perversity that called for remedy and for which Allah sent His Prophet to them? The answer lies in the Qur'ān which demonstrates that the Arabs too suffered from the same mental and attitudinal diseases as had the ancients.

For instance, on the one hand they ascribed participatory divinity with Allah to others, thinking that dominion over casual elements in creation is a shared enterprise involving angels, the righteous, and celestial bodies. On the other hand, in accordance with this perception they worshipped these false gods and invoked them for help to ease their distress. In other words, they too worshipped others beside Allah. Furthermore, they had no concept of Allah as *Rabb*, taking instead their tribal chiefs and family elders as lawmakers.

As regards their suffering from the first disease, the Qur'ān provides the following evidence:

وَمِنَ ٱلنَّاسِ مَن يَعْبُدُ ٱللَّهَ عَلَىٰ حَرْفٍ فَإِنْ أَصَابَهُ خَيْرٌ ٱطْمَأَنَّ بِهِ وَإِنْ أَصَابَتْهُ فِتْنَةٌ ٱنقَلَبَ عَلَىٰ وَجْهِهِ خَسِرَ ٱلدُّنْيَا وَٱلْأَخِرَةَ ذَٰلِكَ هُوَ ٱلْخُسْرَانُ ٱلْمُبِينُ ۞ يَدْعُوا۟ مِن دُونِ ٱللَّهِ مَا لَا يَضُرُّهُ وَمَا لَا يَنفَعُهُ ذَٰلِكَ هُوَ ٱلضَّلَٰلُ ٱلْبَعِيدُ ۞ يَدْعُوا۟ لَمَن ضَرُّهُ أَقْرَبُ مِن نَّفْعِهِ لَبِئْسَ ٱلْمَوْلَىٰ وَلَبِئْسَ ٱلْعَشِيرُ ۞

There are among men some who serve Allah, and (yet stand) on the very fringe (of the true faith). When blessed with good fortune they are well content, but when an ordeal befalls them they turn around, losing this life as well as the Hereafter: that is loss for all to see! They call on such deities, besides Allah, as can neither harm nor profit them: that is straying far indeed (from the Way)! (Perhaps) they call on one whose

hurt is nearer than his profit: evil, indeed, is the patron, and
evil the companion (for help)!

al-Ḥajj 22:11-13

وَيَعْبُدُونَ مِن دُونِ ٱللَّهِ مَا لَا يَضُرُّهُمْ وَلَا يَنفَعُهُمْ وَيَقُولُونَ هَـٰٓؤُلَآءِ
شُفَعَـٰٓؤُنَا عِندَ ٱللَّهِ قُلْ أَتُنَبِّـُٔونَ ٱللَّهَ بِمَا لَا يَعْلَمُ فِى ٱلسَّمَـٰوَٰتِ وَلَا فِى
ٱلْأَرْضِ سُبْحَـٰنَهُۥ وَتَعَـٰلَىٰ عَمَّا يُشْرِكُونَ ۝

They serve, besides Allah, things that hurt them not nor
profit them, and they say: "These are our intercessors with
Allah." Say: "Do you indeed inform Allah of something He
knows not, in the heavens or on earth? – Glory to Him! And
far is He above the partners they ascribe (to Him)!"

Yūnus 10:18

۞ قُلْ أَئِنَّكُمْ لَتَكْفُرُونَ بِٱلَّذِى خَلَقَ ٱلْأَرْضَ فِى يَوْمَيْنِ وَتَجْعَلُونَ لَهُۥٓ أَندَادًا
ذَٰلِكَ رَبُّ ٱلْعَـٰلَمِينَ ۝

Say: Is it that you deny Him Who created the earth in two
days? And do you join equals with Him? He is the Lord of
(all) the worlds.

Fuṣṣilat 41:9

قُلْ أَتَعْبُدُونَ مِن دُونِ ٱللَّهِ مَا لَا يَمْلِكُ لَكُمْ ضَرًّا وَلَا نَفْعًا وَٱللَّهُ هُوَ
ٱلسَّمِيعُ ٱلْعَلِيمُ ۝

Say: "Will you worship, besides Allah, something which has
no power either to harm or benefit you? But Allah – He it is
that hears and knows all things."

al-Māʾidah 5:76

﴿ وَإِذَا مَسَّ ٱلْإِنسَٰنَ ضُرٌّ دَعَا رَبَّهُۥ مُنِيبًا إِلَيْهِ ثُمَّ إِذَا خَوَّلَهُۥ نِعْمَةً مِّنْهُ نَسِيَ
مَا كَانَ يَدْعُوٓاْ إِلَيْهِ مِن قَبْلُ وَجَعَلَ لِلَّهِ أَندَادًا لِّيُضِلَّ عَن سَبِيلِهِۦ قُلْ تَمَتَّعْ
بِكُفْرِكَ قَلِيلًا إِنَّكَ مِنْ أَصْحَٰبِ ٱلنَّارِ ﴾

When some trouble touches man, he cries unto his Lord,
turning to Him in repentance: but when He bestows a
favour upon him as from Himself, (man) forgets what he
cried and prayed for before, and he sets up rivals unto Allah,
thus misleading others from Allah's Path. Say, "Enjoy your
blasphemy for a little while: verily you are (one) of the
companions of the Fire!"

al-Zumar 39:8

وَمَا بِكُم مِّن نِّعْمَةٍ فَمِنَ ٱللَّهِ ثُمَّ إِذَا مَسَّكُمُ ٱلضُّرُّ فَإِلَيْهِ تَجْـَٔرُونَ ۞ ثُمَّ إِذَا
كَشَفَ ٱلضُّرَّ عَنكُمْ إِذَا فَرِيقٌ مِّنكُم بِرَبِّهِمْ يُشْرِكُونَ ۞ لِيَكْفُرُواْ بِمَآ ءَاتَيْنَٰهُمْ
فَتَمَتَّعُواْ فَسَوْفَ تَعْلَمُونَ ۞ وَيَجْعَلُونَ لِمَا لَا يَعْلَمُونَ نَصِيبًا مِّمَّا رَزَقْنَٰهُمْ
تَٱللَّهِ لَتُسْـَٔلُنَّ عَمَّا كُنتُمْ تَفْتَرُونَ ۞

And you have no good thing but is from Allah: and moreover,
when you are touched by distress, unto Him you cry with
groans; yet, when He removes the distress from you, behold!
some of you turn to other gods to join with their Lord – (As
if) to show their ingratitude for the favours We have done to
them! Then enjoy (your brief day); but soon will you know
(your folly)! And they (even) assign, to things they do not
know, a portion out of that which We have bestowed for their
sustenance! By Allah, you shall certainly be called to account
for your false inventions.

al-Naḥl 16:53-56

وَكَذَٰلِكَ زَيَّنَ لِكَثِيرٍ مِّنَ ٱلْمُشْرِكِينَ قَتْلَ أَوْلَٰدِهِمْ شُرَكَآؤُهُمْ لِيُرْدُوهُمْ وَلِيَلْبِسُواْ عَلَيْهِمْ دِينَهُمْ وَلَوْ شَآءَ ٱللَّهُ مَا فَعَلُوهُ فَذَرْهُمْ وَمَا يَفْتَرُونَ ۝

Even so, in the eyes of most of the pagans, their "partners" made alluring the slaughter of their children, in order to lead them to their own destruction, and cause confusion in their religion. If Allah had willed, they would not have done so: but leave alone them and their inventions.

al-An'ām 6:137

Obviously, the expression *shurakā'* (partners) here does not mean idols and gods that they hand crafted but rather those religious people and leaders who made fratricide desirable in Arab eyes conflating that heinous act with the Abrahamic religion. It is also obvious that they did not make them partners with Allah, i.e. as being instrumental in running the affairs of the universe, or that they offered prayers to them and invoked their help. Rather, they arrogated divinity to them, for in their view they had the right to regulate the social, ethical, and religious affairs of their people through laws emanating from their own persons.

أَمْ لَهُمْ شُرَكَٰٓؤُاْ شَرَعُواْ لَهُم مِّنَ ٱلدِّينِ مَا لَمْ يَأْذَنۢ بِهِ ٱللَّهُ وَلَوْلَا كَلِمَةُ ٱلْفَصْلِ لَقُضِىَ بَيْنَهُمْ وَإِنَّ ٱلظَّٰلِمِينَ لَهُمْ عَذَابٌ أَلِيمٌ ۝

What! Have they partners (in godhead), who have established for them some religion without the permission of Allah? Had it not been for the Decree of Judgement, the matter would have been decided between them (at once). But verily the wrongdoers will have a grievous penalty.

al-Shūrā 42:21

We will expand upon the phrase *dīn* later, but here one thing stands resolved: that in bypassing Allah and formulating laws which were of a religious nature which people accepted amounted to associating partners with Allah in His attributes of Divinity and Sovereignty.

The Qur'ānic call

Our research so far has revealed that none of the ancient nations which the Qur'ān describes as usurpers, disbelievers, and deviationists denied their belief in Allah. Nor did they deny Allah's presence or refute His Divinity and His Lordship in the absolute sense. Instead, the perversity common to them all involved splitting divinity into two primary parts.

The meaning of *Rabb* whereby only He has the supernatural ability to nourish, care, satisfy needs, and protect had a different meaning for these peoples. For sure, they believed in Allah's supremacy but along with it, they also believed that the angels, man-made gods, spirits, celestial bodies, prophets, saints, and spiritual guides shared His Divinity.

The second meaning of *Rabb* as the source of all power, guidance, law, sovereignty, and the centre of collective existence also entailed, for them, a different meaning. They took humans as *Rabb* or at best they believed in Allah as their *Rabb* but in practice, they submitted to the moral, cultural and political suzerainty of their own likes.

To correct this degenerative thinking, prophets were sent from the beginning, eventually culminating in the prophetic office of Muḥammad *Rasūl Allāh*. Their unitive call stressed that from all these aspects, Allah the Exalted is the only *Rabb*, that Divinity is indivisible and that not a single aspect of it can be ascribed to anyone but Him. Besides, the universe is a God-centred system created by Him alone; Who is running it all by Himself, with none to share its creation or management. In the religious as well as political sense, Allah alone is humanity's *Rabb*. Thus, He deserves to be the focus of their prayers, needs, and dependence. Likewise, only He could be the Sovereign, the Lawmaker and the Touchstone of right and wrong.

These two aspects of divinity which, because of *jāhilīyah*, humans have splintered into separate entities are peculiar to the essence of divinity. In fact, the two are constitutive of a whole that cannot be separated. Nor can it be justified to associate non-Allah with Allah.

The Qur'ān articulates this prophetic call as follows:

إِنَّ رَبَّكُمُ ٱللَّهُ ٱلَّذِى خَلَقَ ٱلسَّمَـٰوَٰتِ وَٱلْأَرْضَ فِى سِتَّةِ أَيَّامٍ ثُمَّ ٱسْتَوَىٰ عَلَى ٱلْعَرْشِ يُغْشِى ٱلَّيْلَ ٱلنَّهَارَ يَطْلُبُهُۥ حَثِيثًا وَٱلشَّمْسَ وَٱلْقَمَرَ وَٱلنُّجُومَ مُسَخَّرَٰتٍ بِأَمْرِهِۦٓ أَلَا لَهُ ٱلْخَلْقُ وَٱلْأَمْرُ تَبَارَكَ ٱللَّهُ رَبُّ ٱلْعَـٰلَمِينَ ۝

Your Guardian-Lord is Allah, Who created the heavens and the earth in six days, then He established Himself on the Throne (of authority): He draws the night as a veil over the day, each seeking the other in rapid succession: He created the sun, the moon, and the stars, (all) governed by laws under His command. Is it not His to create and to govern? Blessed be Allah, the Cherisher and Sustainer of the worlds!

al-Aʿrāf 7:54

قُلْ مَن يَرْزُقُكُم مِّنَ ٱلسَّمَآءِ وَٱلْأَرْضِ أَمَّن يَمْلِكُ ٱلسَّمْعَ وَٱلْأَبْصَـٰرَ وَمَن يُخْرِجُ ٱلْحَىَّ مِنَ ٱلْمَيِّتِ وَيُخْرِجُ ٱلْمَيِّتَ مِنَ ٱلْحَىِّ وَمَن يُدَبِّرُ ٱلْأَمْرَ فَسَيَقُولُونَ ٱللَّهُ فَقُلْ أَفَلَا تَتَّقُونَ ۝ فَذَٰلِكُمُ ٱللَّهُ رَبُّكُمُ ٱلْحَقُّ فَمَاذَا بَعْدَ ٱلْحَقِّ إِلَّا ٱلضَّلَـٰلُ فَأَنَّىٰ تُصْرَفُونَ ۝

Say: "Who is it that sustains you (in life) from the sky and from the earth? Or Who is it that has power over hearing and sight? And Who is it that brings out the living from the dead and the dead from the living? And Who is it that rules and regulates all affairs?" They will soon say, "Allah". Say, "Will you not then show piety (to Him)?" Such is Allah, your real

Cherisher and Sustainer: apart from Truth, what (remains) but error? How then are you turned away?

Yūnus 10:31-32

خَلَقَ ٱلسَّمَـٰوَٰتِ وَٱلْأَرْضَ بِٱلْحَقِّ يُكَوِّرُ ٱلَّيْلَ عَلَى ٱلنَّهَارِ وَيُكَوِّرُ ٱلنَّهَارَ عَلَى ٱلَّيْلِ وَسَخَّرَ ٱلشَّمْسَ وَٱلْقَمَرَ كُلٌّ يَجْرِى لِأَجَلٍ مُّسَمًّى أَلَا هُوَ ٱلْعَزِيزُ ٱلْغَفَّـٰرُ خَلَقَكُم مِّن نَّفْسٍ وَٰحِدَةٍ ثُمَّ جَعَلَ مِنْهَا زَوْجَهَا وَأَنزَلَ لَكُم مِّنَ ٱلْأَنْعَـٰمِ ثَمَـٰنِيَةَ أَزْوَٰجٍ يَخْلُقُكُمْ فِى بُطُونِ أُمَّهَـٰتِكُمْ خَلْقًا مِّنْ بَعْدِ خَلْقٍ فِى ظُلُمَـٰتٍ ثَلَـٰثٍ ذَٰلِكُمُ ٱللَّهُ رَبُّكُمْ لَهُ ٱلْمُلْكُ لَا إِلَـٰهَ إِلَّا هُوَ فَأَنَّىٰ تُصْرَفُونَ

He created the heavens and the earth in true (proportions): He makes the night overlap the day, and the day overlap the night: He has subjected the sun and the moon (to His law): each one follows a course for time appointed. Is not He the Exalted in Power – He Who forgives again and again? He created you (all) from a single person: then created, of like nature, his mate; and He sent down for you eight head of cattle in pairs: He makes you, in the wombs of your mothers, in stages, one after another, in three veils of darkness. Such is Allah, your Lord and Cherisher: to Him belongs (all) dominion. There is no god but He: then how are you turned away (from your true Centre)?

al-Zumar 39:5-6

اللَّهُ الَّذِى جَعَلَ لَكُمُ الَّيْلَ لِتَسْكُنُوا فِيهِ وَالنَّهَارَ مُبْصِرًا إِنَّ اللَّهَ لَذُو فَضْلٍ
عَلَى النَّاسِ وَلَكِنَّ أَكْثَرَ النَّاسِ لَا يَشْكُرُونَ ۞ ذَٰلِكُمُ اللَّهُ رَبُّكُمْ
خَٰلِقُ كُلِّ شَىْءٍ لَّا إِلَٰهَ إِلَّا هُوَ فَأَنَّىٰ تُؤْفَكُونَ ۞ كَذَٰلِكَ يُؤْفَكُ الَّذِينَ
كَانُوا بِـَٔايَٰتِ اللَّهِ يَجْحَدُونَ ۞ اللَّهُ الَّذِى جَعَلَ لَكُمُ الْأَرْضَ قَرَارًا
وَالسَّمَاءَ بِنَاءً وَصَوَّرَكُمْ فَأَحْسَنَ صُوَرَكُمْ وَرَزَقَكُم مِّنَ الطَّيِّبَٰتِ ذَٰلِكُمُ
اللَّهُ رَبُّكُمْ فَتَبَارَكَ اللَّهُ رَبُّ الْعَٰلَمِينَ ۞ هُوَ الْحَىُّ لَا إِلَٰهَ إِلَّا هُوَ فَادْعُوهُ
مُخْلِصِينَ لَهُ الدِّينَ الْحَمْدُ لِلَّهِ رَبِّ الْعَٰلَمِينَ ۞

It is Allah Who has made the night for you, that you may
rest therein, and the day, as that which helps (you) to see.
Verily Allah is full of Grace and Bounty to men: yet most
men give no thanks. Such is Allah, your Lord, the Creator of
all things. There is no god but He: then how you are deluded
away from the Truth! Thus are deluded those who are wont
to reject the Signs of Allah. It is Allah Who has made for
you the earth as a resting place, and the sky as a canopy, and
has given you shape – and made your shapes beautiful – and
has provided for you Sustenance, of things pure and good
– such is Allah your Lord. So Glory to Allah, the Lord of the
Worlds! He is the Living (One): there is no god but He: call
upon Him, giving Him sincere devotion. Praise be to Allah,
Lord of the Worlds!

al-Mu'min 40:61-65

وَٱللَّهُ خَلَقَكُم مِّن تُرَابٍ ثُمَّ مِن نُّطْفَةٍ ثُمَّ جَعَلَكُمْ أَزْوَٰجًا وَمَا تَحْمِلُ مِنْ

أُنثَىٰ وَلَا تَضَعُ إِلَّا بِعِلْمِهِۦ وَمَا يُعَمَّرُ مِن مُّعَمَّرٍ وَلَا يُنقَصُ مِنْ عُمُرِهِۦٓ إِلَّا فِى

كِتَٰبٍ إِنَّ ذَٰلِكَ عَلَى ٱللَّهِ يَسِيرٌ ۝ وَمَا يَسْتَوِى ٱلْبَحْرَانِ هَٰذَا عَذْبٌ

فُرَاتٌ سَآئِغٌ شَرَابُهُۥ وَهَٰذَا مِلْحٌ أُجَاجٌ وَمِن كُلٍّ تَأْكُلُونَ لَحْمًا طَرِيًّا

وَتَسْتَخْرِجُونَ حِلْيَةً تَلْبَسُونَهَا وَتَرَى ٱلْفُلْكَ فِيهِ مَوَاخِرَ لِتَبْتَغُوا۟ مِن فَضْلِهِۦ

وَلَعَلَّكُمْ تَشْكُرُونَ ۝ يُولِجُ ٱلَّيْلَ فِى ٱلنَّهَارِ وَيُولِجُ ٱلنَّهَارَ فِى ٱلَّيْلِ وَسَخَّرَ

ٱلشَّمْسَ وَٱلْقَمَرَ كُلٌّ يَجْرِى لِأَجَلٍ مُّسَمًّى ذَٰلِكُمُ ٱللَّهُ رَبُّكُمْ لَهُ ٱلْمُلْكُ

وَٱلَّذِينَ تَدْعُونَ مِن دُونِهِۦ مَا يَمْلِكُونَ مِن قِطْمِيرٍ ۝ إِن تَدْعُوهُمْ لَا يَسْمَعُوا۟

دُعَآءَكُمْ وَلَوْ سَمِعُوا۟ مَا ٱسْتَجَابُوا۟ لَكُمْ وَيَوْمَ ٱلْقِيَٰمَةِ يَكْفُرُونَ

بِشِرْكِكُمْ وَلَا يُنَبِّئُكَ مِثْلُ خَبِيرٍ ۝

And Allah did create you from dust; then from a sperm drop;
then He made you in pairs. And no female conceives, or lays
down (her load), but with His knowledge. Nor is a man long-
lived granted length of days, nor is a part cut off from his life,
but is in a decree (ordained). All this is easy for Allah. Nor
are the two bodies of flowing water alike – the one palatable,
sweet, and pleasant to drink, and the other, salty and bitter.
Yet from each (kind of water) do you eat flesh fresh and
tender, and you extract ornaments to wear: and you see the
ships therein that plough the waves, that you may seek (thus)
of the Bounty of Allah that you may be grateful. He merges
night into day, and He merges day into night, and He has
subjected the sun and the moon (to His Law): each one runs
its course for a term appointed. Such is Allah your Lord:
to Him belong all dominion. And those whom you invoke
besides Him have not the least power. If you invoke them,
they will not listen to your call, and if they were to listen,

they cannot answer your (prayer). On the Day of Judgement
they will reject your "partnership". And none, (O man!) can
tell you (the Truth) like the One Who is acquainted with all
things.

Fāṭir 35:11-14

وَلَهُۥ مَن فِى ٱلسَّمَـٰوَٰتِ وَٱلْأَرْضِ كُلٌّ لَّهُۥ قَـٰنِتُونَ ۝ وَهُوَ ٱلَّذِى يَبْدَؤُاْ
ٱلْخَلْقَ ثُمَّ يُعِيدُهُۥ وَهُوَ أَهْوَنُ عَلَيْهِ وَلَهُ ٱلْمَثَلُ ٱلْأَعْلَىٰ فِى ٱلسَّمَـٰوَٰتِ
وَٱلْأَرْضِ وَهُوَ ٱلْعَزِيزُ ٱلْحَكِيمُ ۝ ضَرَبَ لَكُم مَّثَلًا مِّنْ أَنفُسِكُمْ هَل
لَّكُم مِّن مَّا مَلَكَتْ أَيْمَـٰنُكُم مِّن شُرَكَاءَ فِى مَا رَزَقْنَـٰكُمْ فَأَنتُمْ فِيهِ
سَوَآءٌ تَخَافُونَهُمْ كَخِيفَتِكُمْ أَنفُسَكُمْ كَذَٰلِكَ نُفَصِّلُ ٱلْآيَـٰتِ لِقَوْمٍ
يَعْقِلُونَ ۝ بَلِ ٱتَّبَعَ ٱلَّذِينَ ظَلَمُوٓاْ أَهْوَآءَهُم بِغَيْرِ عِلْمٍ فَمَن يَهْدِى مَنْ أَضَلَّ ٱللَّهُ
وَمَا لَهُم مِّن نَّـٰصِرِينَ ۝ فَأَقِمْ وَجْهَكَ لِلدِّينِ حَنِيفًا فِطْرَتَ ٱللَّهِ ٱلَّتِى فَطَرَ
ٱلنَّاسَ عَلَيْهَا لَا تَبْدِيلَ لِخَلْقِ ٱللَّهِ ذَٰلِكَ ٱلدِّينُ ٱلْقَيِّمُ وَلَـٰكِنَّ أَكْثَرَ
ٱلنَّاسِ لَا يَعْلَمُونَ ۝

To Him belongs every being that is in the heavens and on
earth: all are devoutly obedient to Him. It is He Who begins
(the process of) creation; then repeats it; and for Him it is
most easy. To Him belongs the loftiest similitude (we can
think of) in the heavens and the earth: for He is exalted in
Might, full of wisdom. He does propound to you a similitude
from your own (experience): do you have partners among
those whom your right hands possess, to share as equals in
the wealth We have bestowed on you? Do you fear them as
you fear each other? Thus do We explain the Signs in detail
to a people that understand. Nay, the wrongdoers (merely)
follow their own lusts, being devoid of knowledge. But who
will guide those whom Allah leaves astray? To them there will
be no helpers. So set you your face steadily and truly to the

Faith: (establish) Allah's handiwork according to the pattern on which He has made mankind: no change (let there be) in the work (wrought) by Allah: that is the standard Religion: but most among mankind understand not.

al-Rūm 30:26-30

وَمَا قَدَرُوا۟ اللَّهَ حَقَّ قَدْرِهِۦ وَٱلْأَرْضُ جَمِيعًا قَبْضَتُهُۥ يَوْمَ ٱلْقِيَـٰمَةِ وَٱلسَّمَـٰوَٰتُ مَطْوِيَّـٰتٌۢ بِيَمِينِهِۦ سُبْحَـٰنَهُۥ وَتَعَـٰلَىٰ عَمَّا يُشْرِكُونَ ۞

No just estimate have they made of Allah, such as is due to Him: on the Day of Judgement the whole of the earth will be but His handful, and the heavens will be rolled up in His right hand: Glory to Him! High is He above the partners they attribute to Him!

al-Zumar 39:67

فَلِلَّهِ ٱلْحَمْدُ رَبِّ ٱلسَّمَـٰوَٰتِ وَرَبِّ ٱلْأَرْضِ رَبِّ ٱلْعَـٰلَمِينَ ۞ وَلَهُ ٱلْكِبْرِيَآءُ فِى ٱلسَّمَـٰوَٰتِ وَٱلْأَرْضِ وَهُوَ ٱلْعَزِيزُ ٱلْحَكِيمُ ۞

Then Praise be to Allah, Lord of the heavens and Lord of the earth – Lord and Cherisher of all the worlds! To Him be Glory throughout the heavens and the earth: and He is exalted in Power, full of Wisdom!

al-Jāthiyah 45:36-37

رَّبُّ ٱلسَّمَـٰوَٰتِ وَٱلْأَرْضِ وَمَا بَيْنَهُمَا فَٱعْبُدْهُ وَٱصْطَبِرْ لِعِبَـٰدَتِهِۦ هَلْ تَعْلَمُ لَهُۥ سَمِيًّا ۞

"Lord of the heavens and of the earth, and of all that is between them: so worship Him, and be constant and patient in His worship: know you of any who is worthy of the same name as He?"

Maryam 19:65

وَلِلَّهِ غَيْبُ ٱلسَّمَـٰوَٰتِ وَٱلْأَرْضِ وَإِلَيْهِ يُرْجَعُ ٱلْأَمْرُ كُلُّهُ فَٱعْبُدْهُ وَتَوَكَّلْ
عَلَيْهِ وَمَا رَبُّكَ بِغَـٰفِلٍ عَمَّا تَعْمَلُونَ ۞

To Allah belong the unseen (secrets) of the heavens and the
earth, and to Him goes back every affair (for decision): then
worship Him, and put your trust in Him: and your Lord is
not unmindful of aught that you do.

Hūd 11:123

رَّبُّ ٱلْمَشْرِقِ وَٱلْمَغْرِبِ لَآ إِلَـٰهَ إِلَّا هُوَ فَٱتَّخِذْهُ وَكِيلًا ۞

(He is) Lord of the East and the West: there is no god but
He: take Him therefore for (your) Disposer of affairs.

al-Muzzammil 73:9

إِنَّ هَـٰذِهِۦٓ أُمَّتُكُمْ أُمَّةً وَٰحِدَةً وَأَنَا۠ رَبُّكُمْ فَٱعْبُدُونِ ۞ وَتَقَطَّعُوٓا۟ أَمْرَهُم
بَيْنَهُمْ كُلٌّ إِلَيْنَا رَٰجِعُونَ ۞

Verily, this brotherhood of yours is a single brotherhood, and
I am your Lord and Cherisher: therefore serve Me (and no
other). But (later generations) cut off their affairs (of unity),
one from another: (yet) will they all return to Us.

al-Anbiyā' 21:92-93

ٱتَّبِعُوا۟ مَآ أُنزِلَ إِلَيْكُم مِّن رَّبِّكُمْ وَلَا تَتَّبِعُوا۟ مِن دُونِهِۦٓ أَوْلِيَآءَ
قَلِيلًا مَّا تَذَكَّرُونَ ۞

Follow (O men!) the revelation given unto you from your
Lord, and follow not, as friends or protectors, other than
Him. Little it is you remember of admonition.

al-A'rāf 7:3

قُلْ يَـٰٓأَهْلَ ٱلْكِتَـٰبِ تَعَالَوْاْ إِلَىٰ كَلِمَةٍ سَوَآءٍ بَيْنَنَا وَبَيْنَكُمْ أَلَّا نَعْبُدَ
إِلَّا ٱللَّهَ وَلَا نُشْرِكَ بِهِۦ شَيْـًٔا وَلَا يَتَّخِذَ بَعْضُنَا بَعْضًا أَرْبَابًا مِّن دُونِ ٱللَّهِ
فَإِن تَوَلَّوْاْ فَقُولُواْ ٱشْهَدُواْ بِأَنَّا مُسْلِمُونَ ۝

Say: "O People of the Book! Come to common terms as
between us and you: that we worship none but Allah; that
we associate no partners with Him; that we erect not, from
among ourselves, lords and patrons other than Allah." If then
they turn back, say you: "Bear witness that we (at least) are
Muslims (bowing to Allah's Will)."

Āl 'Imrān 3:64

قُلْ أَعُوذُ بِرَبِّ ٱلنَّاسِ ۝ مَلِكِ ٱلنَّاسِ ۝

Say: I seek refuge with the Lord and the Cherisher of
mankind. The King (or Ruler) of mankind.

al-Nās 114:1-2

قُلْ إِنَّمَآ أَنَا۠ بَشَرٌ مِّثْلُكُمْ يُوحَىٰٓ إِلَىَّ أَنَّمَآ إِلَـٰهُكُمْ إِلَـٰهٌ وَٰحِدٌ فَمَن كَانَ
يَرْجُواْ لِقَآءَ رَبِّهِۦ فَلْيَعْمَلْ عَمَلًا صَـٰلِحًا وَلَا يُشْرِكْ بِعِبَادَةِ رَبِّهِۦٓ أَحَدَۢا ۝

Say: "I am but a man like yourselves, (but) the inspiration
has come to me, that your God is One God: whoever expects
to meet his Lord, let him work righteousness, and in the
worship of his Lord, admit no one as partner."

al-Kahf 18:110

By making a sequential reading of these *āyahs*, it becomes obvious
that the Qur'ān equates divinity with sovereignty and dominion. The
Qur'ān projects *al-Rabb* as an Absolute Sovereign with none to share
His ownership and governance.

- It is, thus, in this respect that He is our Provider as well as of the universe, and so is He the Patron and the Solver of our problems.

- It is in this respect that He is our Sustainer, the repository of our trust and our Guardian.

- It is in their respect that our loyalty to Him serves as a natural foundation upon which the edifice of our collective existence is raised. His central position provides a nexus around which divergent groups and people gel into an *ummah*.

- It is in this respect that He deserves our worship and obedience, not just humanity's but all creation's.

- And it is in their respect that He is everybody's Master and Sovereign.

The *jāhilī* Arabs and others in history who shared their mindset, goaded by their misconceptions, splintered this comprehensive notion of divinity into five different divinities conjecturing that diverse people could be invested with them. Nevertheless, the Qur'ān with its powerful rationale blasts away such conjecturing by proving that in a command-centered universe, ruled by a single sovereign, there is no space for others to share divinity with Allah. In fact, the centrality of the system speaks for unicity in the same God Who created it.

Therefore, anyone who ascribes even part of divinity to someone or thing other than Allah in fact fights with reality and denies truth. In this way, he hurts only himself.

'Ibādah

LEXICOGRAPHICALLY, the Arabic words *'ubūdah*, *'ubūdīyah* and *'abdīyah* mean humility, submission, and subjection. To totally surrender to someone offering little or no resistance so that the one who gives in can be used the way the other person wants embraces the total essence of the phrase. The Arabs use the expression *ba'īr mu'abbad* for a camel thoroughly tamed for riding. Likewise, a road flattened by frequent use is called *ṭarīq mu'abbad*. It is from this verbal root that the secondary meanings of slavery, obedience, worship, employment, confinement or obstacle are derived. The prime Arabic dictionary *Lisān al-'Arab*, describes it as follows:

العَبْدُ، المَمْلُوكُ، خِلافُ الحُرِّ

1. *Al-'abd, al-mamlūk khilāf al-ḥurr* – that is, *al-'abd* is someone who is owned by someone else, as opposed to a person who is free (*ḥurr*). Likewise, we say:

تَعَبَّدَ الرَّجُلَ

   ta'abbada al-rajul – meaning to make someone a slave or treat him as a slave.

   The same meaning is carried by *'abbadahū*, *a'bada* and *i'tabadahū*.

2. In one *ḥadīth*, we come across the Prophetic saying:

ثَلاثَةٌ أَنَا خَصْمُهُمْ، رَجُلٌ اعْتَبَدَ مُحَرَّرًا (وفي رِوَايَة عَبْداً مُحَرَّرًا)

thalāthatun anā khaṣmuhum, rajulun i'tabada muḥarraran (wa fī riwāyah 'abdan muḥararran) – meaning, there are three individuals against whom I will rise as prosecutor on Judgement Day. A person, among others, who enslaves a free man or manumits a slave and then treats him like a slave.

The Prophet Mūsā said to Pharaoh:

وَتِلْكَ نِعْمَةٌ تَمُنُّهَا عَلَيَّ أَنْ عَبَّدتَّ بَنِي إِسْرَاءِيلَ

wa tilka ni'matun tamunnuhā 'alayya an 'abbadta Banī Isrā'īl – meaning, and the beneficence that you taunt me with is nothing but [the fact] that you enslaved Banī Isrā'īl.

3.

العِبَادَةُ الطَّاعَةُ مَعَ الخُضُوعِ

Al-'ibādah al-ṭā'ah ma'al-khuḍū' – meaning, worship is obedience faithfully complied with.

عَبَدَ الطَّاغُوتَ، أَيْ أَطَاعَهُ

'Abada al-ṭāghūt ay aṭā'ahū – meaning, [he] worshipped *ṭāghūt* – that is, he became faithful to it.

إِيَّاكَ نَعْبُدُ، أَيْ نُطِيعُ الطَّاعَةَ الَّتِي نَخْضَعُ مَعَهَا

Iyyāka na'budu ... – meaning, You alone we worship, with utmost obedience that it calls for.

أَعْبُدُوا رَبَّكُمْ أَيْ أَطِيْعُوا رَبَّكُمْ

u'budū rabbakum ... – meaning, worship your Lord, that
is, obey Him.

وَقَوْمُهُمَا لَنَا عَابِدُونَ، أَيْ طَائِعُونَ وَكُلُّ مَنْ دَانَ لِمَلِكٍ فَهُوَ عَابِدٌ لَهُ
وَقَالَ إِبْنُ الْأَنْبَارِي: فُلَانٌ عَابِدٌ وَهُوَ الْخَاضِعُ لِرَبِّهِ الْمُسْتَسْلِمُ
الْمُنْقَادُ لِأَمْرِهِ

That is: when Pharaoh said that Moses, and Aaron's
nation was his slave, [he] meant they were bonded to
his will. People who subject themselves to a king's will
become his worshippers – the faithful ones. Ibn al-Anbārī
says, the expression *fulān 'ābid* means he is faithful to
his master and subjects himself to his will.

4.

عَبَدَهُ عِبَادَةً وَمَعْبَدًا وَمَعْبَدَةً تَأَلَّهَ لَهُ

'Abadahū ibādatatn ... – means, he worshipped him
fully.

In the phrase التَّعَبُّدُ التَّنَسُّكُ *al-ta'abbud, al-tanassuk* –
means to adore someone and to become his
worshipper.

A poet once said:

أَرَى الْمَالَ عِنْدَ الْبَاخِلِينَ مُعَبَّدًا

I see money worshipped in stingy people.

In the phrasal expression

عَبَدَهُ وَعَبَدَ بِهِ لَزِمَهُ فَلَمْ يُفَارِقْهُ

'abadahū and *'abada bihī* – means he bonded himself
with him in such a way that never separated from him.

5.

مَا عَبَدَكَ عَنِّي أَيْ مَا حَبَسَكَ

Ma 'abadaka 'annī … – means that when a person stops
going to someone, the latter says: "what prevented you
from coming to me?"

From this explanation, it is obvious that the verbal root *'abd*
signifies accepting someone's superiority and relinquishing freedom,
forsaking resistance and becoming compliant to him. The same goes
for bondage and servitude. A person bonded to his master is supposed
to serve him. Hence obedience is the twin of servitude. It cultivates
itself when a slave not only relegates himself to bondage and obedience
but also believes in his master's superiority, convinced of the latter's
exalted status. He also feels weighed down by his beneficence and
adopts an exaggerated attitude of reverence towards him, performing
in diverse ways the rites of bondage towards his master. Such posturing
and mindset constitute worship.

Expressed differently, this kind of adulation and self-subjection
become worship only when it is not only the slave's head, which he
has lowered in esteem before his master, but his heart as well. As for
bonding one's self to someone else and not parting from them, these
are peripheral concepts, neither real nor fundamental.

'Ibādah in the Qur'ānic lexicon

When we return to the Qur'ān to examine this concept, we find that
the word *'ibādah* is used in the sense of the first three meanings. In
some places, the first and second meanings are used conjointly, while
at other times, only the second or third meanings are employed. The
Qur'ān also uses the word *'ibādah* in a way that conveys all three
meanings.

'Ibādah as bondage and obedience

For example, the following *āyahs* use the expression *'ibādah* in the
context of bondage or slavery and obedience.

ثُمَّ أَرْسَلْنَا مُوسَىٰ وَأَخَاهُ هَـٰرُونَ بِـَٔايَـٰتِنَا وَسُلْطَـٰنٍ مُّبِينٍ ﴿٤٥﴾ إِلَىٰ فِرْعَوْنَ
وَمَلَإِيْهِ فَٱسْتَكْبَرُوا۟ وَكَانُوا۟ قَوْمًا عَالِينَ ﴿٤٦﴾ فَقَالُوٓا۟ أَنُؤْمِنُ لِبَشَرَيْنِ مِثْلِنَا
وَقَوْمُهُمَا لَنَا عَـٰبِدُونَ ﴿٤٧﴾

Then We sent Moses and his brother Aaron, with Our Signs
and authority manifest, to Pharaoh and his Chiefs: but these
behaved insolently: they were an arrogant people. They said:
"Shall we believe in two men like ourselves? And their people
are subject to us!"

al-Mu'minūn 23:45-47

وَتِلْكَ نِعْمَةٌ تَمُنُّهَا عَلَىَّ أَنْ عَبَّدتَّ بَنِىٓ إِسْرَٰٓءِيلَ ﴿٢٢﴾

"And this is the favour with which you do reproach me – that
you have enslaved the Children of Israel!"

al-Shu'arā' 26:22

In both these *āyahs*, '*ibādah* conveys the meaning of subjugation
and obedience.

Pharaoh said Moses' and Aaron's nation was in his servitude
– that is: it was under his writ and abided by it. According to the
āyah, Moses chided Pharaoh for enslaving the Israelites and exacting
labour from them.

يَـٰٓأَيُّهَا ٱلَّذِينَ ءَامَنُوا۟ كُلُوا۟ مِن طَيِّبَـٰتِ مَا رَزَقْنَـٰكُمْ وَٱشْكُرُوا۟ لِلَّهِ إِن
كُنتُمْ إِيَّاهُ تَعْبُدُونَ ﴿١٧٢﴾

O you who believe! Eat of the good things that We have
provided for you and be grateful to Allah, if it is Him you
worship.

al-Baqarah 2:172

The preceding *āyah* was revealed in the context that along with their compliance of the food-related edicts from religious leaders, the post-Islamic Arabs had also adopted their ancestors' superstitious practices. After embracing Islam, Allah asked them to remove these self-inflicted restrictions and eat what had been allowed to them if they truly worshipped Him. Thereby, this implied that they were no longer in the servitude of their priests and ancestors but in Allah's. They would thus, from now on, have to follow the Qur'ānic norms of right and wrong. Even here *'ibādah* is used in the context of servitude and obedience.

قُلْ هَلْ أُنَبِّئُكُم بِشَرٍّ مِّن ذَٰلِكَ مَثُوبَةً عِندَ ٱللَّهِ مَن لَّعَنَهُ ٱللَّهُ وَغَضِبَ عَلَيْهِ وَجَعَلَ مِنْهُمُ ٱلْقِرَدَةَ وَٱلْخَنَازِيرَ وَعَبَدَ ٱلطَّٰغُوتَ أُوْلَٰٓئِكَ شَرٌّ مَّكَانًا وَأَضَلُّ عَن سَوَآءِ ٱلسَّبِيلِ ۝

Say: "Shall I point out to you something much worse than this, (as judged) by the treatment it received from Allah? Those who incurred the curse of Allah and His wrath, those of whom some He transformed into apes and swine, those who worshipped evil – these are (many times) worse in rank, and far more astray from the even path!"

al-Mā'idah 5:60

وَلَقَدْ بَعَثْنَا فِى كُلِّ أُمَّةٍ رَّسُولًا أَنِ ٱعْبُدُواْ ٱللَّهَ وَٱجْتَنِبُواْ ٱلطَّٰغُوتَ فَمِنْهُم مَّنْ هَدَى ٱللَّهُ وَمِنْهُم مَّنْ حَقَّتْ عَلَيْهِ ٱلضَّلَٰلَةُ فَسِيرُواْ فِى ٱلْأَرْضِ فَٱنظُرُواْ كَيْفَ كَانَ عَٰقِبَةُ ٱلْمُكَذِّبِينَ ۝

For We assuredly sent amongst every people a messenger, (with the Command), "Serve Allah, and eschew evil". Of the people were some whom Allah guided, and some on whom error became inevitably (established). So travel through the earth, and see the end of those who denied (the Truth).

al-Naḥl 16:36

$$\text{وَٱلَّذِينَ ٱجْتَنَبُوا۟ ٱلطَّـٰغُوتَ أَن يَعْبُدُوهَا وَأَنَابُوٓا۟ إِلَى ٱللَّهِ لَهُمُ ٱلْبُشْرَىٰ}$$

$$\text{فَبَشِّرْ عِبَادِ ۝}$$

Those who eschew evil – and fall not into its worship – and
turn to Allah (in repentance) – for them is good news: so
announce the Good News to My servants.

al-Zumar 39:17

In all three *āyahs*, people have been warned not to worship *ṭāghūt*.
As already said, in the Qur'ānic lexicon, *ṭāghūt* symbolizes anything
that postures itself outside the Islamic realm in an adversial relationship
to Allah. This includes obtaining a mandate from sources other than
Allah – be it stately, priestly or otherwise and who, by using force,
beat them into subjection or seduce them by money and privileges or
bend them to their writ through subversive education.

'Ibādah as obedience

Let us take the *āyahs* that use the word *'ibādah* in the second sense
of obedience:

$$\text{۞ أَلَمْ أَعْهَدْ إِلَيْكُمْ يَـٰبَنِىٓ ءَادَمَ أَن لَّا تَعْبُدُوا۟ ٱلشَّيْطَـٰنَ ۖ إِنَّهُۥ لَكُمْ}$$

$$\text{عَدُوٌّ مُّبِينٌ ۝}$$

"Did I not enjoin on you, O you Children of Adam, that you
should not worship Satan; for that he was to you an enemy
avowed?"

Yā Sīn 36:60

This *āyah* warns believers about worshipping Shayṭān, which is
seemingly not the case as nobody worships him. Rather, most of the
time we hear people cursing him. Nevertheless, on Judgement Day
humanity will be charged for the crime of following the satanic way
in each and every matter.

۞ ٱحۡشُرُواْ ٱلَّذِينَ ظَلَمُواْ وَأَزۡوَٰجَهُمۡ وَمَا كَانُواْ يَعۡبُدُونَ ۞ مِن دُونِ ٱللَّهِ
فَٱهۡدُوهُمۡ إِلَىٰ صِرَٰطِ ٱلۡجَحِيمِ ۞ وَقِفُوهُمۡۖ إِنَّهُم مَّسۡئُولُونَ ۞ مَا لَكُمۡ
لَا تَنَاصَرُونَ ۞ بَلۡ هُمُ ٱلۡيَوۡمَ مُسۡتَسۡلِمُونَ ۞ وَأَقۡبَلَ بَعۡضُهُمۡ عَلَىٰ بَعۡضٍ
يَتَسَآءَلُونَ ۞ قَالُوٓاْ إِنَّكُمۡ كُنتُمۡ تَأۡتُونَنَا عَنِ ٱلۡيَمِينِ ۞ قَالُواْ بَل لَّمۡ تَكُونُواْ
مُؤۡمِنِينَ ۞ وَمَا كَانَ لَنَا عَلَيۡكُم مِّن سُلۡطَٰنِۢ بَلۡ كُنتُمۡ قَوۡمًا طَٰغِينَ ۞

"Bring them up," it shall be said, "the wrongdoers and their
wives, and the things they worshipped – besides Allah, and
lead them to the way to the (fierce) Fire! But stop them, for
they must be asked: What is the matter with you that you
help not each other?" No, but that day they shall submit (to
Judgement); and they will turn to one another, and question
one another. They will say: "It was you who used to come
to us from the right hand (of power and authority)!" They
will reply: "No, you yourselves had no Faith! Nor had we
any authority over you. No, it was you who were a people in
obstinate rebellion!"

al-Ṣāffāt 37:22-30

This dialogue between the worshippers and their objects of
worship is of special significance. For the gods here are not idols
and icons but rather the priests who, in their disguise of hallowed
spirituality and goodness, became the cause for humanity's deviation,
and who by their rosaries and long dresses trapped people into their
fold of obedience and who by their ostensible calls for reformation
spread mischief in Allah's land. The Qur'ān describes the blind
obedience given to such people as worship ('ibādah).

ٱتَّخَذُوٓاْ أَحۡبَارَهُمۡ وَرُهۡبَٰنَهُمۡ أَرۡبَابًا مِّن دُونِ ٱللَّهِ وَٱلۡمَسِيحَ ٱبۡنَ مَرۡيَمَ
وَمَآ أُمِرُوٓاْ إِلَّا لِيَعۡبُدُوٓاْ إِلَٰهًا وَٰحِدًاۖ لَّآ إِلَٰهَ إِلَّا هُوَۚ سُبۡحَٰنَهُۥ
عَمَّا يُشۡرِكُونَ ۞

They take their priests and their anchorites to be their lords
in derogation of Allah, and (they take as their Lord) Christ,
the son of Mary; yet they were commanded to worship but
One God: there is no god but He. Praise and glory to Him:
(far is He) from having the partners they associate (with
Him).

al-Tawbah 9:31

The Qur'ānic expression "they substituted their clergy and saints
for God..." means they accepted them as the arbiters of right and
wrong in their lives without sanction either from God or His prophet.
Its meaning was amplified by the Prophet Muḥammad himself when
in response to a query from a Christian, that he and his kind never
worshipped clergy or saints, he asked: "Didn't they give preference
to their (priests') words over God's word?"

'Ibādah as ritualistic worship

Now we come to those *āyahs* which amplify the third meaning of
the word *'ibādah*. In the Qur'ān, *'ibādah* as ritual worship entails
two aspects. First, to bow before someone with genuflexion (*rukū'*),
reverential standing (*qiyām*), circumambulation (*ṭawāf*), shrinal
visitation, compensatory offerings and performing sacrificial rites that
are generally associated with worship, notwithstanding whether the
person objectified is taken as a god or as intercessory between the seeker
and the Supreme God or as a partner in the divine enterprise.

Second, it entails perceiving someone as dominant over the causal
world. Such an entity is thereby invoked for the fulfilment of one's
needs, calling on him for the alleviation of one's discomfort, and
seeking protection in him from existential hurt.

The Qur'ān considers these attitudes as falling under the ambit
of worship. For example:

قُلْ إِنِّى نُهِيتُ أَنْ أَعْبُدَ ٱلَّذِينَ تَدْعُونَ مِن دُونِ ٱللَّهِ لَمَّا جَآءَنِىَ ٱلْبَيِّنَـٰتُ
مِن رَّبِّى وَأُمِرْتُ أَنْ أُسْلِمَ لِرَبِّ ٱلْعَـٰلَمِينَ ۝

Say: "I have been forbidden to invoke those whom you invoke besides Allah – seeing that the clear Signs have come to me from my Lord; and I have been commanded to bow (in Islam) to the Lord of the Worlds."

al-Mū'min 40:66

وَأَعْتَزِلُكُمْ وَمَا تَدْعُونَ مِن دُونِ اللَّهِ وَأَدْعُواْ رَبِّى عَسَىٰٓ أَلَّآ أَكُونَ بِدُعَآءِ رَبِّى شَقِيًّا ۞ فَلَمَّا اعْتَزَلَهُمْ وَمَا يَعْبُدُونَ مِن دُونِ اللَّهِ وَهَبْنَا لَهُۥٓ إِسْحَـٰقَ وَيَعْقُوبَ ۖ وَكُلًّا جَعَلْنَا نَبِيًّا ۞

"And I will turn away from you (all) and from those whom you invoke besides Allah: I will call on my Lord: perhaps, by my prayers to my Lord, I shall be not unblest!" When he had turned away from them and from those whom they worshipped besides Allah, We bestowed on him Isaac and Jacob, and each one of them We made a prophet.

Maryam 19:48-49

وَمَنْ أَضَلُّ مِمَّن يَدْعُواْ مِن دُونِ اللَّهِ مَن لَّا يَسْتَجِيبُ لَهُۥٓ إِلَىٰ يَوْمِ الْقِيَـٰمَةِ وَهُمْ عَن دُعَآئِهِمْ غَـٰفِلُونَ ۞ وَإِذَا حُشِرَ النَّاسُ كَانُواْ لَهُمْ أَعْدَآءً وَكَانُواْ بِعِبَادَتِهِمْ كَـٰفِرِينَ ۞

And who is more astray than one who invokes, besides Allah, such as will not answer him till the Day of Judgement, and who (in fact) are unconscious of their call (to them)? And when mankind are gathered together (at the Resurrection), they will be hostile to them and reject their worship (altogether)!

al-Aḥqāf 46:5-6

In the preceding citations, the Qur'ān itself explains that 'ibādah here signifies supplication and invoking help.

قَالُواْ سُبْحَـٰنَكَ أَنتَ وَلِيُّنَا مِن دُونِهِمۖ بَلْ كَانُواْ يَعْبُدُونَ ٱلْجِنَّ أَكْثَرُهُم بِهِم مُّؤْمِنُونَ ۝

They will say, "Glory to You! Our (tie) is with You – as Protector – not with them. No, but they worshipped the *jinn*: most of them believed in them."

Saba' 34:41

Worshipping *jinn* and believing in their ability to help humans may sound bizarre but the Qur'ān itself explains it as follows:

وَأَنَّهُۥ كَانَ رِجَالٌ مِّنَ ٱلْإِنسِ يَعُوذُونَ بِرِجَالٍ مِّنَ ٱلْجِنِّ فَزَادُوهُمْ رَهَقًا ۝

True, there were persons among mankind who took shelter with persons among the *jinn*, but they increased them in folly.

al-Jinn 72:6

We thus know that worshipping *jinn* means seeking their protection against danger and loss, while believing in them means they have the power to provide humans with a protective shield from the vagaries of life.

وَيَوْمَ يَحْشُرُهُمْ وَمَا يَعْبُدُونَ مِن دُونِ ٱللَّهِ فَيَقُولُ ءَأَنتُمْ أَضْلَلْتُمْ عِبَادِى هَـٰٓؤُلَآءِ أَمْ هُمْ ضَلُّواْ ٱلسَّبِيلَ ۝ قَالُواْ سُبْحَـٰنَكَ مَا كَانَ يَنۢبَغِى لَنَآ أَن نَّتَّخِذَ مِن دُونِكَ مِنْ أَوْلِيَآءَ وَلَـٰكِن مَّتَّعْتَهُمْ وَءَابَآءَهُمْ حَتَّىٰ نَسُواْ ٱلذِّكْرَ وَكَانُواْ قَوْمًۢا بُورًا ۝

The Day He will gather them together as well as those whom they worship besides Allah, He will ask "Was it you who led these My servants astray. Or did they stray from the Path themselves?" They will say: "Glory to You! It was not our meet to take other guardians besides You."

al-Furqān 25:17-18

In these *āyahs*, the narrative style has a tonal directness that tells all – self-made gods include those saints and spiritual guides whom their followers endowed with divinity thinking, in their naivety, that they could help them in their hour of need. In this way, they gave them respect, accompanied by physical posturing of abnegation and obeisance normally only identified with worship.

The Qur'ān further explains this worship concept in the following *āyah*:

وَيَوْمَ يَحْشُرُهُمْ جَمِيعًا ثُمَّ يَقُولُ لِلْمَلَـٰئِكَةِ أَهَـٰٓؤُلَاءِ إِيَّاكُمْ كَانُوا۟ يَعْبُدُونَ ۝ قَالُوا۟ سُبْحَـٰنَكَ أَنتَ وَلِيُّنَا مِن دُونِهِم ۖ بَلْ كَانُوا۟ يَعْبُدُونَ ٱلْجِنَّ ۖ أَكْثَرُهُم بِهِم مُّؤْمِنُونَ ۝

One Day He will gather them all together, and say to the angels, "Was it you that these men used to worship?" They will say, "Glory to You! Our (tie) is with You – as Protector – not with them. No, but they worshipped the *jinn*: most of them believed in them."

Saba' 34:40-41

Here, the phrase angel-worship stands for that imaginative figuration of angels which people handcraft out of reverence and awe so that by placating them they invite their attention towards their problems and, thus, seek spiritual redress.

وَيَعْبُدُونَ مِن دُونِ ٱللَّهِ مَا لَا يَضُرُّهُمْ وَلَا يَنفَعُهُمْ وَيَقُولُونَ هَـٰٓؤُلَاءِ شُفَعَـٰٓؤُنَا عِندَ ٱللَّهِ ۚ قُلْ أَتُنَبِّئُونَ ٱللَّهَ بِمَا لَا يَعْلَمُ فِى ٱلسَّمَـٰوَٰتِ وَلَا فِى ٱلْأَرْضِ ۚ سُبْحَـٰنَهُۥ وَتَعَـٰلَىٰ عَمَّا يُشْرِكُونَ ۝

They serve, besides Allah, things that hurt them not nor
profit them, and they say: "These are our intercessors with
Allah." Say: "Do you indeed inform Allah of something He
knows not, in the heavens or on earth? – Glory to Him! And
far is He above the partners they ascribe (to Him)!"

Yūnus 10:18

أَلَا لِلَّهِ ٱلدِّينُ ٱلْخَالِصُ وَٱلَّذِينَ ٱتَّخَذُوا۟ مِن دُونِهِۦ أَوْلِيَآءَ مَا نَعْبُدُهُمْ
إِلَّا لِيُقَرِّبُونَآ إِلَى ٱللَّهِ زُلْفَىٰٓ إِنَّ ٱللَّهَ يَحْكُمُ بَيْنَهُمْ فِى مَا هُمْ فِيهِ يَخْتَلِفُونَ إِنَّ
ٱللَّهَ لَا يَهْدِى مَنْ هُوَ كَـٰذِبٌ كَفَّارٌ ۞

Is it not to Allah that sincere devotion is due? But those who
take for protectors others than Allah (say): "We only serve
them in order that they may bring us nearer to Allah." Truly
Allah will judge between them in that wherein they differ.
But Allah guides not such as are false and ungrateful.

al-Zumar 39:3

Even here, in these Qur'ānic citations, '*ibādah* means worshipping
someone either because people attribute intercessory powers to them,
or because they think that the person objectified as god can bring
them closer to Allah.

'*Ibādah* as servitude, obedience and worship
The preceding illustrations amplify the point that sometimes the
Qur'ān uses the expression '*ibādah* in the sense of servitude and
surrender, and sometimes in the abstract sense of compliance and
adoration. Before we cite textual situations in which '*ibādah* embraces
all three shades of meaning, it is important for readers to understand
our premise.

In the examples given so far, we have citations of people who
worshipped individuals and angels rather than Allah. At places where
'*ibādah* is reduced to aspects of servitude and obedience, the god

objectified is either Satan or seditious humans who wear the emblem of *ṭāghūt* and thereby seduced others to their worship. Included among this group are leaders and saints that have led people astray, by inclining them towards their self-made codes of law.

In cases where *'ibādah* means worship, human-made gods are either prophets, saints, or the pious who have been elevated as such by flying in the face of their teachings. Or they are from among the angels and *jinn* who have mistakenly been bestowed with divinity in the supernatural sense. Alternatively, they represent the anthropomorphized figuration of natural forces satanically installed as objects of worship. The Qur'ān demolishes all such artificial gods as false and their *'ibādah* wrong, no matter what form it takes – whether of servitude, compliance or ritualistic worship. It unequivocally declares that the gods people make are in fact Allah's bonded slaves. They have neither the right to call others to their worship nor will anyone receive anything from them except humiliation and disappointment. For Allah alone is the Master of this universe, He alone holds power and, thus, other than Him none qualifies as deserving worship.

إِنَّ ٱلَّذِينَ تَدْعُونَ مِن دُونِ ٱللَّهِ عِبَادٌ أَمْثَالُكُمْ فَٱدْعُوهُمْ فَلْيَسْتَجِيبُوا۟ لَكُمْ إِن كُنتُمْ صَـٰدِقِينَ ۝ أَلَهُمْ أَرْجُلٌ يَمْشُونَ بِهَآ أَمْ لَهُمْ أَيْدٍ يَبْطِشُونَ بِهَآ أَمْ لَهُمْ أَعْيُنٌ يُبْصِرُونَ بِهَآ أَمْ لَهُمْ ءَاذَانٌ يَسْمَعُونَ بِهَا قُلِ ٱدْعُوا۟ شُرَكَآءَكُمْ ثُمَّ كِيدُونِ فَلَا تُنظِرُونِ ۝ إِنَّ وَلِـِّۧىَ ٱللَّهُ ٱلَّذِى نَزَّلَ ٱلْكِتَـٰبَ وَهُوَ يَتَوَلَّى ٱلصَّـٰلِحِينَ ۝ وَٱلَّذِينَ تَدْعُونَ مِن دُونِهِ لَا يَسْتَطِيعُونَ نَصْرَكُمْ وَلَآ أَنفُسَهُمْ يَنصُرُونَ ۝

Verily those whom you call upon besides Allah are servants like unto you: call upon them, and let them listen to your prayer, if you are (indeed) truthful! Have they feet to walk with? Or hands to lay hold with? Or eyes to see with? Or ears to hear with? Say: "Call your 'god-partners', scheme (your worst) against me, and give me no respite! For my Protector

is Allah, Who revealed the Book (from time to time), and
He will choose and befriend the righteous. But those you
call upon besides Him are unable to help you, and indeed to
help themselves."

al-A'rāf 7:194-197

وَقَالُواْ ٱتَّخَذَ ٱلرَّحْمَـٰنُ وَلَدًا سُبْحَـٰنَهُۥ بَلْ عِبَادٌ مُّكْرَمُونَ ۞ لَا يَسْبِقُونَهُۥ بِٱلْقَوْلِ وَهُم بِأَمْرِهِۦ يَعْمَلُونَ ۞ يَعْلَمُ مَا بَيْنَ أَيْدِيهِمْ وَمَا خَلْفَهُمْ وَلَا يَشْفَعُونَ إِلَّا لِمَنِ ٱرْتَضَىٰ وَهُم مِّنْ خَشْيَتِهِۦ مُشْفِقُونَ ۞

And they say: "(Allah) Most Gracious has begotten offspring."
Glory to Him! They are (but) servants raised to honour. They
speak not before He speaks, and they act (in all things) by
His command. He knows what is before them, and what is
behind them, and they offer no intercession except for those
who are acceptable, and they stand in awe and reverence of
His (Glory).

al-Anbiyā' 21:26-28

وَجَعَلُوا ٱلْمَلَـٰئِكَةَ ٱلَّذِينَ هُمْ عِبَـٰدُ ٱلرَّحْمَـٰنِ إِنَـٰثًا أَشَهِدُواْ خَلْقَهُمْ سَتُكْتَبُ شَهَـٰدَتُهُمْ وَيُسْـَٔلُونَ ۞

And they make into females angels who themselves serve
Allah. Did they witness their creation? Their evidence will
be recorded, and they will be called to account!

al-Zukhruf 43:19

وَجَعَلُواْ بَيْنَهُۥ وَبَيْنَ ٱلْجِنَّةِ نَسَبًا وَلَقَدْ عَلِمَتِ ٱلْجِنَّةُ إِنَّهُمْ لَمُحْضَرُونَ ۞

And they have invented a blood-relationship between Him
and the *jinn*: but the *jinn* know (quite well) that they have
indeed to appear (before His Judgement Seat)!

al-Ṣāffāt 37:158

لَّن يَسْتَنكِفَ ٱلْمَسِيحُ أَن يَكُونَ عَبْدًا لِّلَّهِ وَلَا ٱلْمَلَـٰٓئِكَةُ ٱلْمُقَرَّبُونَ وَمَن يَسْتَنكِفْ عَنْ عِبَادَتِهِ وَيَسْتَكْبِرْ فَسَيَحْشُرُهُمْ إِلَيْهِ جَمِيعًا ۝

Christ disdains not to serve and worship Allah, nor do the angels, those nearest (to Allah): those who disdain His worship and are arrogant – He will gather them all together unto Himself to (answer).

al-Nisā' 4:172

ٱلشَّمْسُ وَٱلْقَمَرُ بِحُسْبَانٍ ۝ وَٱلنَّجْمُ وَٱلشَّجَرُ يَسْجُدَانِ ۝

The sun and the moon follow courses (exactly) computed; and the herbs and the trees both (alike) bow in adoration.

al-Raḥmān 55:5-6

تُسَبِّحُ لَهُ ٱلسَّمَـٰوَٰتُ ٱلسَّبْعُ وَٱلْأَرْضُ وَمَن فِيهِنَّ وَإِن مِّن شَىْءٍ إِلَّا يُسَبِّحُ بِحَمْدِهِ وَلَـٰكِن لَّا تَفْقَهُونَ تَسْبِيحَهُمْ إِنَّهُ كَانَ حَلِيمًا غَفُورًا ۝

The seven heavens and the earth, and all beings therein, declare His Glory: there is not a thing but celebrates His praise: and you understand not how they declare His Glory! Verily He is Oft-Forbearing, Most Forgiving!

al-Isrā' 17:44

وَلَهُۥ مَن فِى ٱلسَّمَـٰوَٰتِ وَٱلْأَرْضِ كُلٌّ لَّهُۥ قَـٰنِتُونَ ۝

To Him belongs every being that is in the heavens and on earth: all are devoutly obedient to Him.

al-Rūm 30:26

إِنِّى تَوَكَّلْتُ عَلَى ٱللَّهِ رَبِّى وَرَبِّكُم مَّا مِن دَآبَّةٍ إِلَّا هُوَ ءَاخِذٌۢ بِنَاصِيَتِهَآ إِنَّ رَبِّى عَلَىٰ صِرَٰطٍ مُّسْتَقِيمٍ ۝

"I put my trust in Allah, my Lord and your Lord! There is not a moving creature, but He hath grasp of its forelock. Verily, it is my Lord that is on a straight Path."

Hūd 11:56

إِن كُلُّ مَن فِى ٱلسَّمَٰوَٰتِ وَٱلْأَرْضِ إِلَّآ ءَاتِى ٱلرَّحْمَٰنِ عَبْدًا ۝ لَّقَدْ أَحْصَىٰهُمْ وَعَدَّهُمْ عَدًّا ۝ وَكُلُّهُمْ ءَاتِيهِ يَوْمَ ٱلْقِيَٰمَةِ فَرْدًا ۝

Not one of the beings in the heavens and the earth but must come to (Allah) Most Gracious as a servant. He does take an account of them (all) and has numbered them (all) exactly. And every one of them will come to Him singly on the Day of Judgement.

Maryam 19:93-95

قُلِ ٱللَّهُمَّ مَٰلِكَ ٱلْمُلْكِ تُؤْتِى ٱلْمُلْكَ مَن تَشَآءُ وَتَنزِعُ ٱلْمُلْكَ مِمَّن تَشَآءُ وَتُعِزُّ مَن تَشَآءُ وَتُذِلُّ مَن تَشَآءُ بِيَدِكَ ٱلْخَيْرُ إِنَّكَ عَلَىٰ كُلِّ شَىْءٍ قَدِيرٌ ۝

Say: "O Allah! Lord of Power (and Rule), You give power to whom You please, and You strip off power from whom You please: You exalt whom You please, and You bring low whom You please: in Your hand is all good. Verily, over all things You have power."

Āl 'Imrān 3:26

The Qur'ān establishes the diminutive rank of self-made gods, and then demands that humans as well as *jinn* worship Allah alone. As such, if there is any servitude, obedience or ritualistic worship, it should be of Allah only. Not even the slightest element of such worship should be for anyone else.

وَلَقَدْ بَعَثْنَا فِي كُلِّ أُمَّةٍ رَّسُولًا أَنِ ٱعْبُدُوا۟ ٱللَّهَ وَٱجْتَنِبُوا۟ ٱلطَّـٰغُوتَ ۖ فَمِنْهُم مَّنْ هَدَى ٱللَّهُ وَمِنْهُم مَّنْ حَقَّتْ عَلَيْهِ ٱلضَّلَـٰلَةُ ۚ فَسِيرُوا۟ فِي ٱلْأَرْضِ فَٱنظُرُوا۟ كَيْفَ كَانَ عَـٰقِبَةُ ٱلْمُكَذِّبِينَ ۝

For We assuredly sent amongst every people a messenger, (with the Command), "Serve Allah, and eschew evil": of the people were some whom Allah guided, and some on whom error became inevitably (established). So travel through the earth, and see the end of those who denied (the Truth).

al-Naḥl 16:36

وَٱلَّذِينَ ٱجْتَنَبُوا۟ ٱلطَّـٰغُوتَ أَن يَعْبُدُوهَا وَأَنَابُوٓا۟ إِلَى ٱللَّهِ لَهُمُ ٱلْبُشْرَىٰ ۚ فَبَشِّرْ عِبَادِ ۝

Those who eschew evil – and fall not into its worship – and turn to Allah (in repentance) – for them is Good News: so announce the good news to My servants –

al-Zumar 39:17

۞ أَلَمْ أَعْهَدْ إِلَيْكُمْ يَـٰبَنِىٓ ءَادَمَ أَن لَّا تَعْبُدُوا۟ ٱلشَّيْطَـٰنَ ۖ إِنَّهُۥ لَكُمْ عَدُوٌّ مُّبِينٌ ۝ وَأَنِ ٱعْبُدُونِى ۚ هَـٰذَا صِرَٰطٌ مُّسْتَقِيمٌ ۝

"Did I not enjoin on you, O you children of Adam, that you should not worship Satan; for that he was to you an enemy avowed? – And that you should worship Me, (for that) this was the straight Way?"

Yā Sīn 36:60-61

اَتَّخَذُوٓاْ أَحْبَارَهُمْ وَرُهْبَٰنَهُمْ أَرْبَابًا مِّن دُونِ ٱللَّهِ وَٱلْمَسِيحَ ٱبْنَ مَرْيَمَ
وَمَآ أُمِرُوٓاْ إِلَّا لِيَعْبُدُوٓاْ إِلَٰهًا وَٰحِدًا ۖ لَّآ إِلَٰهَ إِلَّا هُوَ ۚ سُبْحَٰنَهُۥ
عَمَّا يُشْرِكُونَ ۝

They take their priests and their anchorites to be their lords
in derogation of Allah, and (they take as their Lord) Christ,
the son of Mary; yet they were commanded to worship but
One God: there is no god but He. Praise and glory to Him:
(far is He) from having the partners they associate (with
Him).

al-Tawbah 9:31

يَٰٓأَيُّهَا ٱلَّذِينَ ءَامَنُواْ كُلُواْ مِن طَيِّبَٰتِ مَا رَزَقْنَٰكُمْ وَٱشْكُرُواْ لِلَّهِ إِن
كُنتُمْ إِيَّاهُ تَعْبُدُونَ ۝

O you who believe! Eat of the good things that We have
provided for you and be grateful to Allah, if it is Him you
worship.

al-Baqarah 2:172

In these uncluttered and transparent *āyahs* people are being told
that when it comes to *'ibādah* in the sense of servitude and obedience,
it should be for Allah alone. They should desist from following *ṭāghūt*,
Shayṭān, clergy, and their ancestors.

وَقَالَ رَبُّكُمُ ٱدْعُونِىٓ أَسْتَجِبْ لَكُمْ ۚ إِنَّ ٱلَّذِينَ يَسْتَكْبِرُونَ عَنْ عِبَادَتِى
سَيَدْخُلُونَ جَهَنَّمَ دَاخِرِينَ ۝

And your Lord says: "Call on Me; I will answer your (prayer):
but those who are too arrogant to serve Me will surely find
themselves in Hell – in humiliation!"

al-Mu'min 40:60

قُلْ إِنِّى نُهِيتُ أَنْ أَعْبُدَ ٱلَّذِينَ تَدْعُونَ مِن دُونِ ٱللَّهِ لَمَّا جَآءَنِى ٱلْبَيِّنَتُ مِن رَّبِّى وَأُمِرْتُ أَنْ أُسْلِمَ لِرَبِّ ٱلْعَٰلَمِينَ ۞

Say: "I have been forbidden to invoke those whom you invoke besides Allah – seeing that the clear Signs have come to me from my Lord; and I have been commanded to bow (in Islam) to the Lord of the Worlds."

al-Mu'min 40:66

يُولِجُ ٱلَّيْلَ فِى ٱلنَّهَارِ وَيُولِجُ ٱلنَّهَارَ فِى ٱلَّيْلِ وَسَخَّرَ ٱلشَّمْسَ وَٱلْقَمَرَ كُلٌّ يَجْرِى لِأَجَلٍ مُّسَمًّى ذَٰلِكُمُ ٱللَّهُ رَبُّكُمْ لَهُ ٱلْمُلْكُ وَٱلَّذِينَ تَدْعُونَ مِن دُونِهِ مَا يَمْلِكُونَ مِن قِطْمِيرٍ ۞ إِن تَدْعُوهُمْ لَا يَسْمَعُوا۟ دُعَآءَكُمْ وَلَوْ سَمِعُوا۟ مَا ٱسْتَجَابُوا۟ لَكُمْ وَيَوْمَ ٱلْقِيَٰمَةِ يَكْفُرُونَ بِشِرْكِكُمْ وَلَا يُنَبِّئُكَ مِثْلُ خَبِيرٍ ۞

He merges night into day, and He merges day into night, and He has subjected the sun and the moon (to His Law): each one runs its course for a term appointed. Such is Allah your Lord: to Him belongs all dominion. And those whom you invoke besides Him have not the least power. If you invoke them, they will not listen to your call, and if they were to listen, they cannot answer your (prayer). On the Day of Judgement they will reject your "partnership". And none, (O man!) can tell you (the Truth) like the One Who is acquainted with all things.

Fāṭir 35:13-14

قُلْ أَتَعْبُدُونَ مِن دُونِ ٱللَّهِ مَا لَا يَمْلِكُ لَكُمْ ضَرًّا وَلَا نَفْعًا وَٱللَّهُ هُوَ ٱلسَّمِيعُ ٱلْعَلِيمُ ۞

Say: "Will you worship, besides Allah, something which has
no power either to harm or benefit you? But Allah – He it is
that hears and knows all things."

al-Mā'idah 5:76

In these *āyahs*, *'ibādah* is equalized with reverential attitudes
hymning someone's name for help. These *āyahs* as well as the ones
that follow, talk about those self-crafted gods that have been associated
with Allah in the supernatural sense of His being.

It should not be difficult now to understand that whenever the
Qur'ān talks about worshipping Allah without reducing it to any
particular meaning, *'ibādah* entails servitude, obedience, and ritual
worship. For example:

$$إِنِّى أَنَا۠ رَبُّكَ فَٱخْلَعْ نَعْلَيْكَ إِنَّكَ بِٱلْوَادِ ٱلْمُقَدَّسِ طُوًى ۝$$

"Verily I am your Lord! Therefore (in My presence) put off
your shoes: (for) you are in the sacred valley Ṭuwā."

Ṭā Hā 20:12

$$ذَٰلِكُمُ ٱللَّهُ رَبُّكُمْ لَآ إِلَٰهَ إِلَّا هُوَ خَٰلِقُ كُلِّ شَىْءٍ فَٱعْبُدُوهُ وَهُوَ عَلَىٰ كُلِّ شَىْءٍ وَكِيلٌ ۝$$

That is Allah, your Lord! There is no god but He, the Creator
of all things; then worship you Him; and He has power to
dispose of all affairs.

al-An'ām 6:102

$$قُلْ يَٰٓأَيُّهَا ٱلنَّاسُ إِن كُنتُمْ فِى شَكٍّ مِّن دِينِى فَلَآ أَعْبُدُ ٱلَّذِينَ تَعْبُدُونَ مِن دُونِ ٱللَّهِ وَلَٰكِنْ أَعْبُدُ ٱللَّهَ ٱلَّذِى يَتَوَفَّىٰكُمْ وَأُمِرْتُ أَنْ أَكُونَ مِنَ ٱلْمُؤْمِنِينَ ۝$$

Say "O you men! If you are in doubt as to my religion,
(behold!) I worship not what you worship other than Allah!
But I worship Allah – Who will take your souls (at death): I
am commanded to be (in the ranks) of the believers."

Yūnus 10:104

مَا تَعْبُدُونَ مِن دُونِهِۦٓ إِلَّآ أَسْمَآءً سَمَّيْتُمُوهَآ أَنتُمْ وَءَابَآؤُكُم مَّآ أَنزَلَ ٱللَّهُ
بِهَا مِن سُلْطَٰنٍ إِنِ ٱلْحُكْمُ إِلَّا لِلَّهِ أَمَرَ أَلَّا تَعْبُدُوٓا۟ إِلَّآ إِيَّاهُ ذَٰلِكَ ٱلدِّينُ
ٱلْقَيِّمُ وَلَٰكِنَّ أَكْثَرَ ٱلنَّاسِ لَا يَعْلَمُونَ ۝

"If not Him, you worship nothing but names which you have
named – you and your fathers – for which Allah has sent
down no authority: the command is for none but Allah: He
has commanded that you worship none but Him: that is the
right religion, but most men understand not…"

Yūsuf 12:40

وَلِلَّهِ غَيْبُ ٱلسَّمَٰوَٰتِ وَٱلْأَرْضِ وَإِلَيْهِ يُرْجَعُ ٱلْأَمْرُ كُلُّهُۥ فَٱعْبُدْهُ وَتَوَكَّلْ
عَلَيْهِ وَمَا رَبُّكَ بِغَٰفِلٍ عَمَّا تَعْمَلُونَ ۝

To Allah belong the unseen (secrets) of the heavens and the
earth, and to Him goes back every affair (for decision): then
worship Him, and put your trust in Him: and your Lord is
not unmindful of aught that you do.

Hūd 11:123

وَمَا نَتَنَزَّلُ إِلَّا بِأَمْرِ رَبِّكَ لَهُۥ مَا بَيْنَ أَيْدِينَا وَمَا خَلْفَنَا وَمَا بَيْنَ ذَٰلِكَ
وَمَا كَانَ رَبُّكَ نَسِيًّا ۝ رَّبُّ ٱلسَّمَٰوَٰتِ وَٱلْأَرْضِ وَمَا بَيْنَهُمَا فَٱعْبُدْهُ
وَٱصْطَبِرْ لِعِبَٰدَتِهِۦ هَلْ تَعْلَمُ لَهُۥ سَمِيًّا ۝

(The angels say:) "We descend not but by command of your
Lord: to Him belongs what is before us, and what is behind

us, and what is between: and your Lord never does forget"
– "Lord of the heavens and of the earth, and of all that is
between them: so worship Him, and be constant and patient
in His worship: do you know of any who is worthy of the
same name as He?"

Maryam 19:64-65

قُل إِنَّمَآ أَنَا۠ بَشَرٌ مِّثْلُكُمْ يُوحَىٰٓ إِلَيَّ أَنَّمَآ إِلَٰهُكُمْ إِلَٰهٌ وَٰحِدٌ فَمَن كَانَ
يَرْجُوا۟ لِقَآءَ رَبِّهِۦ فَلْيَعْمَلْ عَمَلًا صَٰلِحًا وَلَا يُشْرِكْ بِعِبَادَةِ رَبِّهِۦٓ أَحَدًا ۝

Say: "I am but a man like yourselves, (but) the inspiration
has come to me, that your God is One God: whoever expects
to meet his Lord, let him work righteousness, and, in the
worship of his Lord, admit no one as partner."

al-Kahf 18:110

Thus, there is no reason to confine the word *'ibādah* in these
āyahs to a ritualistic praxis or servitude and obeisance. In such *āyahs*,
the Qur'ān is presenting its whole *da'wah*. It impresses upon us that
we should surrender to Allah in all aspects of *'ibādah*.

Obviously, to make such *āyahs* restrictive in their import is to
restrict the Qur'ānic message. Unless such ideas are clarified, people
who embrace Islam do so with an acute disability; they are unable to
follow the Qur'ān in its wholeness.

Dīn

IN THE Arabic lexicon the phrase *dīn* is used in diverse ways. For example, it is employed in the sense of sovereignty to restrain someone into submission and compliance. For instance, people say in Arabic:

دَانَ النَّاسَ أَيْ قَهَرَهُمْ عَلَى الطَّاعَةِ

That is: people were forced into compliance.

دِنْتُهُمْ فَدَانُوْا أَيْ قَهَرْتُهُمْ فَأَطَاعُوْا

That is: I subjugated them and they became compliant.

دِنْتُ القَوْمَ أَيْ ذَلَّلْتُهُمْ واستَعْبَدْتُّهُمْ

That is: I overpowered a certain people and made them subservient.

دَانَ الرَّجُلُ إِذَا عَزَّ

That is: a certain person acquired respect and power.

دِنْتُ الرَّجُلَ حَمَلْتُهُ عَلَى مَا يَكْرَهُ

That is: I forced him to do something for which he was not willing.

دِيْنَ فُلَانٍ إِذَا حُمِلَ عَلَى مَا مَكْرُوْهٍ

That is: he was constrained to do this work.

دِنْتُهُ إِذَا سُسْتُهُ ومَلَكْتُهُ

That is: I subjected him to my writ and overwhelmed him.

دِيْنتُهُ الْقَوْمَ ووَلَّيْتُهُ سِيَاسَتَهُمْ

That is: I delegated power to him to rule over people.

In this same sense, Ḥutīyah addresses his mother:

لَقَدْ دَيَّنْتِ أَمْرَ بَنِيكَ حَتَّى
تَرَكْتِهِمْ أَدَقَّ مِنَ الطَّحِينِ

meaning: your children were entrusted to your care but you grinded them even thinner than the wheat flour.

A *ḥadīth* says:

الكَيِّسُ مَنْ دَانَ نَفْسَهُ وَعَمِلَ لِمَا بَعْدَ الْمَوْتِ

That is: a person is wise if he tames his own self (*nafs*) and does what is profitable for him in the *Ākhirah* (Hereafter).

In a similar sense, a person is known as *dayyān* if he overwhelms and dominates a nation, a country, or a people, and they follow his writ.

Thus, Aʿshā al-Ḥarmāzī addressed the Prophet (*ṣallal-Lāhu ʿalayhi wa-sallam*) as:

ياسيّد النّاس وديّان العرب

Yā Sayyid al-Nās wa dayyān al-ʿArab – that is, the master of the people and leader of the Arab.

In the same sense, *madīn* conveys the meaning of being a slave while *madīnah* means a slave-girl. Likewise, Ibn Madīnah stands for the son of a slave-girl. Says Akhṭal:

رَبَّتْ وَرَبَّانِيْ حِجْرُهَا ابْنُ مَدِينَةٍ

A slave girl raised me, I was raised in her lap.

As opposed to this, the Qur'ān poses the ultimate question to its readers: if you are not in bondage to someone (Allah), then why don't you save the dying one from death? Why don't you recall life into him?

وَنَحْنُ أَقْرَبُ إِلَيْهِ مِنكُمْ وَلَـٰكِن لَّا تُبْصِرُونَ ۞ فَلَوْلَا إِن كُنتُمْ غَيْرَ مَدِينِينَ ۞ تَرْجِعُونَهَا إِن كُنتُمْ صَادِقِينَ ۞

But We are nearer to him than you, and yet see not – then why do you not – if you are exempt from (future) account – call back the soul if you are true.

al-Wāqiʿah 56:85-87

In its other aspect, *dīn* stands for obedience, servitude, and compliance. It also means to subject one's self to someone and follow him – that is, to surrender to somebody's power and transcendence. In Arabic they say:

دِنْتُهُمْ فَدَانُوْا أَيْ قَهَرْتُهُمْ فَأَطَاعُوْا

"I have overwhelmed them and they have become compliant."

Likewise, they say:

دِنْتُ الرَّجُلَ أَيْ خَدِمْتُهُ

Dintu al-rajula ay khadimtuhū – that is, I served him.

One *ḥadīth* also employs the expression *tadīnu*:

أُرِيْدُ مِنْ قُرَيْشٍ كَلِمَةً تَدِيْنُ لَهُمْ بِهَا الْعَرَبُ أَيْ تُطِيعُهُمْ وَتَخْضَعُ لَهُمْ

That is: I want the Quraysh to uphold a *kalimah* which if they embrace, the whole of Arabia will submit to their will.

In the same vein, a conforming people are called *qawm dayyin*. The following *ḥadīth* relating to the Khawārij conveys this same meaning.

يَمْرُقُوْنَ مِنَ الدِّيْنِ مُرُوْقَ السَّهْمِ مِنَ الرَّمِيَّة

They slip out of religion as an arrow slips out of the bow.

In its third aspect, it stands for the *Sharī'ah*, law, method, the *ummah* or people, usage and custom. For instance:

مَا زَالَ ذَلِكَ دِيْنِي وَدَيْدَنِيْ

That is: this always had been my way.

Again in the construction

يُقَالُ دَانَ إِذَا اعْتَادَ خَيْرًا وَشَرًّا

This means that a person may follow a bad or a good way.

Nevertheless, in both cases whatever may be his chosen path it will be described as *dīn*.

One *ḥadīth* says:

كَانَتْ قُرَيْشٌ وَمَنْ دَانَ دِيْنَهُمْ

meaning the Quraysh and those who follow their way.

In yet another *ḥadīth* the word *'alā-dīn* is used in almost the same sense:

إِنَّهُ عَلَيْهِ السَّلَامَ كَانَ عَلَى دِيْنِ قَوْمِهِ

innahū 'alayhis salām kāna 'alā dīni qawmihī – means that before his elevation to the prophetic office the Prophet Muḥammad followed the way of his people. Meaning thereby that in marriage, divorce, inheritance and other cultural and social issues, he was obliged to follow the same rules and regulations that were then in practice.

In its fourth aspect, *dīn* stands for reward deeds, accountability and decision. Thus, it is said in Arabic

كَمَا تَدِيْنُ تُدَانُ

as you sow, so do you reap. In the same vein, the Qur'ān articulates the nonbelievers' reaction to the reality of post-death accountability in these words: *a'innā lamadīnūn...*

أَءِنَّا لَمَدِيْنُوْنَ

meaning after death are we going to be subjected to accountability and be paid back?

'Abdullāh ibn 'Umar reports that the Prophet (*'alayhis salām*) said:

لاَتَسُبُّوْا السُّلْطَانَ فَإِنْ كَانَ لاَ بُدَّ فَقُوْلُوْا اللَّهُمَّ دِنْهُمْ كَمَا يَدِيْنُوْنَ

meaning do not call your rulers by bad names. If you have to say something then say: "O Allah, treat them the way they treat us."

Likewise, the word *dayyān* is used for a *qāḍī* or judge. Thus, when someone was asked about 'Alī (Allah be pleased with him), the person described him كَانَ دَيَّانْ هَذِه الأُمَّة بَعْدَ نَبِيَّهَا the greatest of all *qāḍīs* after the Prophet.

Qur'ānic usage of the word *dīn*
By now we know that the word *dīn* entails four concepts. Or we may say that in the Arabic language it conveys four foundational concepts:

* The dominion and control of the powerful.
* Obeisance, surrender, and compliance by one who has accepted the dominion of the person in power.
* Rules, regulations and a code that a person has to comply with.
* Accountability, verdict, punishment, and reward.

The pre-Islamic Arabs used these concepts in different situations. But since their understanding of these concepts was partially cluttered and relatively un-sublime, the use of the word *dīn* carried a certain imprecision. With the revelation of the Qur'ān, however, the expression *al-dīn* assumed a phrasal precision, becoming a foundational term with a known profile. *Al-dīn* thus embraced and still does a whole life system that has four ingredients to it:

• Governance and sovereignty

• Obeisance and surrender as opposed to governance and sovereignty.

• A system of thought and life that develops under its dominion and control.

• Dispensation of punishments and rewards in lieu of loyalty to the given system or non-compliance and rebellion against it.

Sometimes, Qur'ānic usage of the word *dīn* is confined to the first and second meanings; sometimes, it is restricted to its third or fourth expressions. And occasionally, it uses *dīn* in the sense of the whole system, i.e. that which entails all four meanings. To illustrate our point, we invite you to look at the following *āyahs*:

اللَّهُ ٱلَّذِى جَعَلَ لَكُمُ ٱلْأَرْضَ قَرَارًا وَٱلسَّمَآءَ بِنَآءً وَصَوَّرَكُمْ فَأَحْسَنَ صُوَرَكُمْ وَرَزَقَكُم مِّنَ ٱلطَّيِّبَٰتِ ذَٰلِكُمُ ٱللَّهُ رَبُّكُمْ فَتَبَارَكَ ٱللَّهُ رَبُّ ٱلْعَٰلَمِينَ ۞ هُوَ ٱلْحَىُّ لَآ إِلَٰهَ إِلَّا هُوَ فَٱدْعُوهُ مُخْلِصِينَ لَهُ ٱلدِّينَ ٱلْحَمْدُ لِلَّهِ رَبِّ ٱلْعَٰلَمِينَ ۞

It is Allah Who has made for you the earth as a resting place, and the sky as a canopy, and has given you shape – and made your shapes beautiful – and has provided for you Sustenance, of things pure and good – such is Allah your Lord. So Glory be to Allah, the Lord of the Worlds! He is the Living (One): there is no god but He: call upon Him, giving Him sincere devotion. Praise be to Allah, Lord of the Worlds!

al-Mu'min 40:64-65

قُلْ إِنِّي أُمِرْتُ أَنْ أَعْبُدَ ٱللَّهَ مُخْلِصًا لَّهُ ٱلدِّينَ ۞ وَأُمِرْتُ لِأَنْ أَكُونَ أَوَّلَ ٱلْمُسْلِمِينَ ۞ قُلْ إِنِّي أَخَافُ إِنْ عَصَيْتُ رَبِّي عَذَابَ يَوْمٍ عَظِيمٍ ۞ قُلِ ٱللَّهَ أَعْبُدُ مُخْلِصًا لَّهُ دِينِي ۞ فَٱعْبُدُوا مَا شِئْتُم مِّن دُونِهِ قُلْ إِنَّ ٱلْخَـٰسِرِينَ ٱلَّذِينَ خَسِرُوا أَنفُسَهُمْ وَأَهْلِيهِمْ يَوْمَ ٱلْقِيَـٰمَةِ أَلَا ذَٰلِكَ هُوَ ٱلْخُسْرَانُ ٱلْمُبِينُ ۞ لَهُم مِّن فَوْقِهِمْ ظُلَلٌ مِّنَ ٱلنَّارِ وَمِن تَحْتِهِمْ ظُلَلٌ ذَٰلِكَ يُخَوِّفُ ٱللَّهُ بِهِ عِبَادَهُ يَـٰعِبَادِ فَٱتَّقُونِ ۞ وَٱلَّذِينَ ٱجْتَنَبُوا ٱلطَّـٰغُوتَ أَن يَعْبُدُوهَا وَأَنَابُوا إِلَى ٱللَّهِ لَهُمُ ٱلْبُشْرَىٰ فَبَشِّرْ عِبَادِ ۞

Say: "Verily, I am commanded to serve Allah with sincere devotion; and I am commanded to be the first of those who bow to Allah in Islam." Say: "I would, if I disobeyed my Lord, indeed have fear of the Penalty of a Mighty Day." Say: "It is Allah I serve, with my sincere (and exclusive) devotion: Serve you what you will besides Him." Say: "Truly, those in loss are those who lose their own souls and their people on the Day of Judgement: Ah! That is indeed the (real and) evident Loss!" They shall have Layers of Fire above them, and Layers (of Fire) below them: with this Does Allah warn off His servants: "O My servants! Then fear you Me!" Those who eschew Evil – and fall not into its worship – and turn to Allah (in repentance) – for them is Good News: so announce the Good News to My servants –

al-Zumar 39:11-17

إِنَّآ أَنزَلْنَآ إِلَيْكَ ٱلْكِتَـٰبَ بِٱلْحَقِّ فَٱعْبُدِ ٱللَّهَ مُخْلِصًا لَّهُ ٱلدِّينَ ۝ أَلَا لِلَّهِ
ٱلدِّينُ ٱلْخَالِصُ ۚ وَٱلَّذِينَ ٱتَّخَذُوا۟ مِن دُونِهِۦٓ أَوْلِيَآءَ مَا نَعْبُدُهُمْ إِلَّا لِيُقَرِّبُونَآ
إِلَى ٱللَّهِ زُلْفَىٰٓ إِنَّ ٱللَّهَ يَحْكُمُ بَيْنَهُمْ فِى مَا هُمْ فِيهِ يَخْتَلِفُونَ ۗ إِنَّ ٱللَّهَ لَا يَهْدِى
مَنْ هُوَ كَـٰذِبٌ كَفَّارٌ ۝

We have sent down the Book to you with truth. So, worship Allah, making religion exclusive for Him. Is it not to Allah that sincere devotion is due? But those who take for protectors others than Allah (say): "We only serve them in order that they may bring us nearer to Allah." Truly Allah will judge between them in that wherein they differ. But Allah guides not such as are false and ungrateful.

al-Zumar 39:2-3

وَلَهُۥ مَا فِى ٱلسَّمَـٰوَٰتِ وَٱلْأَرْضِ وَلَهُ ٱلدِّينُ وَاصِبًا ۚ أَفَغَيْرَ ٱللَّهِ تَتَّقُونَ ۝

To Him belongs whatever is in the heavens and on earth. And to Him is duty due always: then will you fear other than Allah?

al-Naḥl 16:52

أَفَغَيْرَ دِينِ ٱللَّهِ يَبْغُونَ وَلَهُۥٓ أَسْلَمَ مَن فِى ٱلسَّمَـٰوَٰتِ وَٱلْأَرْضِ طَوْعًا وَكَرْهًا
وَإِلَيْهِ يُرْجَعُونَ ۝

Do they seek for other than the Religion of Allah? – while all creatures in the heavens and on earth have, willing or unwilling, bowed to His Will (accepted Islam), and to Him shall they all be brought back.

Āl ʿImrān 3:83

وَمَآ أُمِرُوٓاْ إِلَّا لِيَعْبُدُواْ ٱللَّهَ مُخْلِصِينَ لَهُ ٱلدِّينَ حُنَفَآءَ وَيُقِيمُواْ ٱلصَّلَوٰةَ وَيُؤْتُواْ ٱلزَّكَوٰةَ وَذَٰلِكَ دِينُ ٱلْقَيِّمَةِ ۞

And they have been commanded no more than this: to worship
Allah, offering Him sincere devotion, being true (in faith);
to establish regular prayers; and to practise regular Charity;
and that is the Religion Right and Straight.

al-Bayyinah 98:5

In all these *āyahs* the word *dīn* is used in the sense of accepting
the authority of the Sovereign with corresponding compliance of His
commands. To purify religion for Allah means a believer must not
recognize the dominion, control, and governance of any person other
than Allah. Likewise, while distancing himself from other bondages,
he should give his obeisance and servitude to Allah alone.

Dīn in the sense of an all-embracing life system

قُلْ يَـٰٓأَيُّهَا ٱلنَّاسُ إِن كُنتُمْ فِى شَكٍّ مِّن دِينِى فَلَآ أَعْبُدُ ٱلَّذِينَ تَعْبُدُونَ مِن دُونِ ٱللَّهِ وَلَـٰكِنْ أَعْبُدُ ٱللَّهَ ٱلَّذِى يَتَوَفَّىٰكُمْ وَأُمِرْتُ أَنْ أَكُونَ مِنَ ٱلْمُؤْمِنِينَ ۞ وَأَنْ أَقِمْ وَجْهَكَ لِلدِّينِ حَنِيفًا وَلَا تَكُونَنَّ مِنَ ٱلْمُشْرِكِينَ ۞

Say: "O you men! If you are in doubt as to my religion,
(behold)! I worship not what you worship, other than Allah!
But I worship Allah – Who will take your souls (at death):
I am commanded to be (in the ranks) of the Believers, and
further (thus): 'set your face toward religion with true piety,
and never in anyway be of the Unbelievers.'"

Yūnus 10:104–105

مَا تَعْبُدُونَ مِن دُونِهِ إِلَّآ أَسْمَآءً سَمَّيْتُمُوهَآ أَنتُمْ وَءَابَآؤُكُم مَّآ أَنزَلَ ٱللَّهُ
بِهَا مِن سُلْطَانٍ إِنِ ٱلْحُكْمُ إِلَّا لِلَّهِ أَمَرَ أَلَّا تَعْبُدُوٓاْ إِلَّآ إِيَّاهُ ذَٰلِكَ ٱلدِّينُ
ٱلْقَيِّمُ وَلَـٰكِنَّ أَكْثَرَ ٱلنَّاسِ لَا يَعْلَمُونَ ۝

"If not Him, you worship nothing but names which you have
named – you and your fathers – for which Allah has sent
down no authority: the command is for none but Allah: He
has commanded that you worship none but Him: that is the
right religion, but most men understand not …"

Yūsuf 12:40

وَلَهُۥ مَن فِى ٱلسَّمَـٰوَٰتِ وَٱلْأَرْضِ كُلٌّ لَّهُۥ قَـٰنِتُونَ ۝ وَهُوَ ٱلَّذِى يَبْدَؤُاْ
ٱلْخَلْقَ ثُمَّ يُعِيدُهُۥ وَهُوَ أَهْوَنُ عَلَيْهِ وَلَهُ ٱلْمَثَلُ ٱلْأَعْلَىٰ فِى ٱلسَّمَـٰوَٰتِ
وَٱلْأَرْضِ وَهُوَ ٱلْعَزِيزُ ٱلْحَكِيمُ ۝ ضَرَبَ لَكُم مَّثَلًا مِّنْ أَنفُسِكُمْ هَلْ
لَّكُم مِّن مَّا مَلَكَتْ أَيْمَـٰنُكُم مِّن شُرَكَآءَ فِى مَا رَزَقْنَـٰكُمْ فَأَنتُمْ فِيهِ
سَوَآءٌ تَخَافُونَهُمْ كَخِيفَتِكُمْ أَنفُسَكُمْ كَذَٰلِكَ نُفَصِّلُ ٱلْآيَـٰتِ لِقَوْمٍ
يَعْقِلُونَ ۝ بَلِ ٱتَّبَعَ ٱلَّذِينَ ظَلَمُوٓاْ أَهْوَآءَهُم بِغَيْرِ عِلْمٍ فَمَن يَهْدِى مَنْ أَضَلَّ ٱللَّهُ
وَمَا لَهُم مِّن نَّـٰصِرِينَ ۝ فَأَقِمْ وَجْهَكَ لِلدِّينِ حَنِيفًا فِطْرَتَ ٱللَّهِ ٱلَّتِى فَطَرَ
ٱلنَّاسَ عَلَيْهَا لَا تَبْدِيلَ لِخَلْقِ ٱللَّهِ ذَٰلِكَ ٱلدِّينُ ٱلْقَيِّمُ وَلَـٰكِنَّ أَكْثَرَ
ٱلنَّاسِ لَا يَعْلَمُونَ ۝

To Him belongs every being that is in the heavens and on
earth: all are devoutly obedient to Him. It is He Who begins
(the process of) creation; then repeats it; and for Him it is
most easy. To Him belongs the loftiest similitude (we can
think of) in the heavens and the earth: for He is Exalted in
Might, full of wisdom. He does propound to you a similitude

from your own (experience): do you have partners among
those whom your right hands possess, to share as equals in
the wealth We have bestowed on you? Do you fear them as
you fear each other? Thus do We explain the Signs in detail
to a people that understand. Nay, the wrongdoers (merely)
follow their own lusts, being devoid of knowledge but who
will guide those whom Allah leaves astray? To them there
will be no helpers. So set your face steadily and truly to the
Faith: (establish) Allah's handiwork according to the pattern
on which He has made mankind: no change (let there be) in
the work (wrought) by Allah: that is the standard Religion:
but most among mankind understand not.

al-*Rūm* 30:26-30

ٱلزَّانِيَةُ وَٱلزَّانِى فَٱجْلِدُواْ كُلَّ وَٰحِدٍ مِّنْهُمَا مِاْئَةَ جَلْدَةٍ وَلَا تَأْخُذْكُم بِهِمَا
رَأْفَةٌ فِى دِينِ ٱللَّهِ إِن كُنتُمْ تُؤْمِنُونَ بِٱللَّهِ وَٱلْيَوْمِ ٱلْءَاخِرِ وَلْيَشْهَدْ عَذَابَهُمَا
طَآئِفَةٌ مِّنَ ٱلْمُؤْمِنِينَ ۝

The woman and the man guilty of adultery or fornication –
flog each of them with a hundred stripes: let not compassion
move you in their case, in a matter prescribed by Allah, if
you believe in Allah and the Last Day: and let a party of the
Believers witness their punishment.

al-*Nūr* 24:2

إِنَّ عِدَّةَ ٱلشُّهُورِ عِندَ ٱللَّهِ ٱثْنَا عَشَرَ شَهْرًا فِى كِتَٰبِ ٱللَّهِ يَوْمَ خَلَقَ ٱلسَّمَٰوَٰتِ
وَٱلْأَرْضَ مِنْهَآ أَرْبَعَةٌ حُرُمٌ ذَٰلِكَ ٱلدِّينُ ٱلْقَيِّمُ فَلَا تَظْلِمُواْ فِيهِنَّ أَنفُسَكُمْ
وَقَٰتِلُواْ ٱلْمُشْرِكِينَ كَآفَّةً كَمَا يُقَٰتِلُونَكُمْ كَآفَّةً وَٱعْلَمُوٓاْ أَنَّ ٱللَّهَ مَعَ
ٱلْمُتَّقِينَ ۝

The number of months in the sight of Allah is twelve (in a
year) – so ordained by Him the day He created the heavens
and the earth; of them four are sacred: that is the straight
usage. So wrong not yourselves therein, and fight the pagans
all together as they fight you all together. But know that Allah
is with those who restrain themselves.

al-Tawbah 9:36

فَبَدَأَ بِأَوْعِيَتِهِمْ قَبْلَ وِعَآءِ أَخِيهِ ثُمَّ ٱسْتَخْرَجَهَا مِن وِعَآءِ أَخِيهِ ۚ كَذَٰلِكَ
كِدْنَا لِيُوسُفَ ۖ مَا كَانَ لِيَأْخُذَ أَخَاهُ فِى دِينِ ٱلْمَلِكِ إِلَّا أَن يَشَآءَ ٱللَّهُ ۚ نَرْفَعُ
دَرَجَٰتٍ مَّن نَّشَآءُ ۗ وَفَوْقَ كُلِّ ذِى عِلْمٍ عَلِيمٌ ۝

So he began (the search) with their baggage, before (he came
to) the baggage of his brother: at length he brought it out
of his brother's baggage. Thus did We plan for Joseph. He
could not take his brother by the law of the king except that
Allah willed it (so). We raise to degrees (of wisdom) whom
We please: but over all endued with knowledge is One, the
All-Knowing.

Yūsuf 12:76

وَكَذَٰلِكَ زَيَّنَ لِكَثِيرٍ مِّنَ ٱلْمُشْرِكِينَ قَتْلَ أَوْلَٰدِهِمْ شُرَكَآؤُهُمْ لِيُرْدُوهُمْ
وَلِيَلْبِسُواْ عَلَيْهِمْ دِينَهُمْ ۖ وَلَوْ شَآءَ ٱللَّهُ مَا فَعَلُوهُ ۖ فَذَرْهُمْ وَمَا يَفْتَرُونَ ۝

Even so, in the eyes of most of the pagans, their "partners"
made alluring the slaughter of their children, in order to lead
them to their own destruction, and cause confusion in their
religion. If Allah had willed, they would not have done so:
but leave alone them and their inventions.

al-An'ām 6:137

أَمْ لَهُمْ شُرَكَـٰٓؤُاْ شَرَعُواْ لَهُم مِّنَ ٱلدِّينِ مَا لَمْ يَأْذَنۢ بِهِ ٱللَّهُ وَلَوْلَا كَلِمَةُ ٱلْفَصْلِ لَقُضِىَ بَيْنَهُمْ وَإِنَّ ٱلظَّـٰلِمِينَ لَهُمْ عَذَابٌ أَلِيمٌ ۝

What! Have they partners (in godhead), who have established
for them some religion without the permission of Allah? Had
it not been for the Decree of Judgement, the matter would
have been decided between them (at once). But verily the
wrongdoers will have a grievous penalty.

al-Shūrā 42:21

لَكُمْ دِينُكُمْ وَلِىَ دِينِ ۝

To you be your way, and to me mine.

al-Kāfirūn 109:6

In all these *āyahs*, the expression *dīn* stands for law, code, the
Sharīʿah, method, and system of thought and a praxis by which
humans live their collective existence. For example, if the dominion
that gives authenticity to a code or a system that binds people into
collectivity is Allah specific, then they are in His *dīn*.

On the other hand, if the dominion and governance belong to a
certain king, then humans are in his *dīn*. If it is owned by the priestly
class or a clan, or by a nation, then the people are in their *dīn*. In short,
if a people accept and abide by the authority from which power flows
and from which the system derives its sanction, then technically, as
well as in reality, they are followers of that authority's *dīn*.

Dīn in the sense of accountability

إِنَّمَا تُوعَدُونَ لَصَادِقٌ ۞ وَإِنَّ ٱلَّذِينَ لَوَاقِعٌ ۞

Verily that which you are promised is true; and verily
Judgement and Justice must indeed come to pass.

al-Dhāriyāt 51:5-6

أَرَءَيْتَ ٱلَّذِى يُكَذِّبُ بِٱلدِّينِ ۞ فَذَٰلِكَ ٱلَّذِى يَدُعُّ ٱلْيَتِيمَ ۞ وَلَا يَحُضُّ
عَلَىٰ طَعَامِ ٱلْمِسْكِينِ ۞

Have you thought of him who denies the Judgement (to
come)? Then such is the (man) who repulses the orphan (with
harshness), and encourages not the feeding of the indigent.

al-Māʿūn 107:1-3

وَمَآ أَدْرَىٰكَ مَا يَوْمُ ٱلدِّينِ ۞ ثُمَّ مَآ أَدْرَىٰكَ مَا يَوْمُ ٱلدِّينِ ۞ يَوْمَ لَا تَمْلِكُ
نَفْسٌ لِّنَفْسٍ شَيْـًٔا ۖ وَٱلْأَمْرُ يَوْمَئِذٍ لِّلَّهِ ۞

And what will explain to you what the Day of Judgement is?
Again, what will explain to you what the Day of Judgement
is? (It will be) the Day when no soul shall have power (to
do) aught for another: for the command, that Day, will be
(wholly) with Allah.

al-Infiṭār 82:17-19

The comprehensive terminology of *dīn*

By looking into the meaning of these *āyahs*, it is obvious that the
Qur'ān uses the word *dīn* in almost the same sense that the Arabs
used it in common parlance. Subsequently, however, as the revelatory
message continued its descent, the Qur'ān gave the expression

terminological precision. The Qur'ān equates *dīn* with a system of
life wherein humans accept someone as sovereign and then follow him
in all aspects without reservation, harmonizing their lives to his laws
in the hope of receiving compensation on compliance while fearing
him for his humiliation and punishment on noncompliance. Perhaps
no other language holds in its vocabulary a word of such amplitude
and fullness as is *dīn*.

Present-day usage of the word "state" has appropriated its
meaning to a certain extent, though to reach its fullness calls for more
space than we have here. In the following *dīn* is used in the sense of
a state.

قَـٰتِلُواْ ٱلَّذِينَ لَا يُؤْمِنُونَ بِٱللَّهِ وَلَا بِٱلْيَوْمِ ٱلْأَخِرِ وَلَا يُحَرِّمُونَ مَا حَرَّمَ ٱللَّهُ
وَرَسُولُهُۥ وَلَا يَدِينُونَ دِينَ ٱلْحَقِّ مِنَ ٱلَّذِينَ أُوتُواْ ٱلْكِتَـٰبَ حَتَّىٰ يُعْطُواْ
ٱلْجِزْيَةَ عَن يَدٍ وَهُمْ صَـٰغِرُونَ ۝

Fight those who believe not in Allah nor the Last Day, nor
hold that forbidden which has been forbidden by Allah and
His Messenger, nor acknowledge the Religion of Truth, from
among the People of the Book, until they pay the *jizyah* with
willing submission, and feel themselves subdued.

al-Tawbah 9:29

Here, the expression *dīn al-ḥaqq* carries a terminological essence,
which Allah the Exalted Himself described in the prefatory sentence as
disbelief in His sole Sovereignty, in the last Judgement and disputation
of His laws of right and wrong.

وَقَالَ فِرْعَوْنُ ذَرُونِىٓ أَقْتُلْ مُوسَىٰ وَلْيَدْعُ رَبَّهُۥٓ إِنِّىٓ أَخَافُ أَن يُبَدِّلَ دِينَكُمْ
أَوْ أَن يُظْهِرَ فِى ٱلْأَرْضِ ٱلْفَسَادَ ۝

Said Pharaoh: "Leave me to slay Moses; and let him call on his Lord! What I fear is lest he should change your religion or lest he should cause mischief to appear in the land!"

al-Mu'min 40:26

The Pharaoh-Moses conflict, as described in the Qur'ān, obviates any doubt that the word *dīn* here does not stand for religion in its abstract form but in the sense of a state and a system. Pharaoh held that if Moses succeeded in his mission, the state structure would undergo change undoing the then system and laws. Either the prevalent set-up would be replaced by a new one based on different values, or in the absence of any system the nation would recede into chaos.

وَمَن يَبْتَغِ غَيْرَ ٱلْإِسْلَٰمِ دِينًا فَلَن يُقْبَلَ مِنْهُ وَهُوَ فِي ٱلْآخِرَةِ مِنَ ٱلْخَٰسِرِينَ ۝

If anyone desires a religion other than Islam (submission to Allah), it will never be accepted of him; and in the Hereafter he will be in the ranks of those who have lost (all spiritual good).

Āl 'Imrān 3:85

هُوَ ٱلَّذِىٓ أَرْسَلَ رَسُولَهُۥ بِٱلْهُدَىٰ وَدِينِ ٱلْحَقِّ لِيُظْهِرَهُۥ عَلَى ٱلدِّينِ كُلِّهِۦ وَلَوْ كَرِهَ ٱلْمُشْرِكُونَ ۝

It is He Who has sent His Messenger with guidance and the Religion of Truth, to proclaim it over all religion, even though the pagans may detest (it).

al-Tawbah 9:33

وَقَٰتِلُوهُمْ حَتَّىٰ لَا تَكُونَ فِتْنَةٌ وَيَكُونَ ٱلدِّينُ كُلُّهُۥ لِلَّهِ فَإِنِ ٱنتَهَوْا۟ فَإِنَّ ٱللَّهَ بِمَا يَعْمَلُونَ بَصِيرٌ ۝

And fight them on until there is no more tumult or oppression, and there prevails justice and faith in Allah altogether and everywhere; but if they cease, verily Allah does see all that they do.

al-Anfāl 8:39

إِذَا جَآءَ نَصْرُ ٱللَّهِ وَٱلْفَتْحُ ۞ وَرَأَيْتَ ٱلنَّاسَ يَدْخُلُونَ فِى دِينِ ٱللَّهِ أَفْوَاجًا ۞
فَسَبِّحْ بِحَمْدِ رَبِّكَ وَٱسْتَغْفِرْهُ إِنَّهُۥ كَانَ تَوَّابًا ۞

When comes the help of Allah, and victory, and you see the people enter Allah's Religion in crowds, celebrate the praises of the Lord, and pray for His forgiveness: for He is Oft-Returning (in Grace and Mercy).

al-Naṣr 110:1-3

In the preceding *āyahs,* the term *dīn* means the entire system of life hinged on dogma, ritual praxis, substantive norms, concepts, morals, and practical aspects.

The first *āyah* holds that in Allah's sight the right course of life is based on compliance with Allah's law. No other system which is marked by obeisance to some other hypothetical power holder is acceptable to the Lord of the universe. This has its support in *fiṭrah* (nature) as well as in logic and common sense. How can the God Who created humans and nurtured them to life and growth in His kingdom allow them discretion to live under someone else's dominion and control?

In the second *āyah,* Allah the Exalted says that He has sent His Messenger with the perfect way of life with the assigned task of making it prevail over other systems.

In the third *āyah,* Islam's followers are told to fight in Allah's way until mischief and rebellion are subdued, ungodly systems are replaced, and humans are brought back into His fold in servitude and compliance.

74

162 :: *Four Key Concepts of the Qur'ān*

The fourth *āyah* capsulates the occasion when, after 23 years of hard, consistent labour, the Islamic change had fructified. Islam in all its glory of a full-fledged system embracing beliefs, thoughts, morals, civilizational and political aspects was established. Arab delegates from the four corners of the Arabian Peninsula had begun to trek towards Madīnah and enter the system. Thus, the task accomplished and for which the Prophet (*'alayhis salām*) was picked by Allah the Exalted, the Qur'ān then brings home the lesson by telling the Prophet not to attribute success to his own efforts. Nor should he feel proud for it is Allah alone Who is perfect, free from blemish. Praise is for Him. So the Prophet Muḥammed too is advised to seek His forgiveness for lapses that might have taken place during the 23 years he spent in discharging his obligations.